KU-780-416

DEC. PAT. 1.

DECORATIVE PATTERNS

OF THE

ANCIENT WORLD

BY

FLINDERS PETRIE, Kt., F.R.S., F.B.A.

STUDIO EDITIONS
LONDON

First published 1930

This edition published in 1990 by Studio Editions
an imprint of Studio Editions Ltd, Princess House,
50 Eastcastle Street, London W1N 7AP, England

Copyright this edition © Studio Editions 1990

All rights reserved. No part of this publication
may be reproduced, stored in a retrieval system,
or transmitted, in any form or by any means, electronic,
mechanical, photocopying, recording or otherwise,
without the prior permission of the copyright holder.

Printed and bound in Czechoslovakia

ISBN 1 85170 359 4

DECORATIVE PATTERNS

OF THE

ANCIENT WORLD.

The purpose of this collection is historical, and any interests that it may claim by racial characters or charms of form are only by the way. It stands as a first outline of an index to all the decorative imaginings of man. The subject is boundless, and to wait for completion would bar any useful result. This beginning of an arrangement of the matter will serve for sorting new material into a form in which it can be compared, registered and consulted.

The limitations of the subject in this volume are where it would trench on ground which is sufficiently known already. The course of civilizations since A.D. 1000 are so far familiar that the artistic connections would not add to our history of events; the architectural studies of capitals and mouldings are so many that they form an entire subject, well-worked, which would overbalance the general history of decoration if included here; the whole theory of interlacing (ACM) or the enormous mass of mosaics in the Roman world seldom add a new form; the many long trails of degradation of forms, human, animal, and vegetable, are usually of little value, as such subjects may equally well be adopted by any people, and simplification usually follows. Geographically this series is limited to Europe and Western Asia, with their links to other lands, but ignoring designs which are special to Siberia, China, or India.

The value of decoration, historically, is due to its having no stimulus of necessity. Where an invention is obviously needed, man will repeatedly invent on much the same lines, to meet his wants. But there is no general need fulfilled by drawing a spiral, rather than a triangle or an octopus. There is great diversity of fertility in different peoples; some abound in fresh ideas—like the Cretans or Apulians, others are limited to two or three stock devices—as the Babylonians or Chinese. The historic connections of design that can be traced, with due regard to place and period, give a strong presumption of a real connection between the designers. This may be due to descent, which will revive a forgotten style after it has been overlaid—like Late Celtic, under Louis Quinze (see LY 96); or it may be a racial movement, like the spread of Hellenism in Asia; or by trade connections—as the Mykenaean style in Egypt, or Chinese in England; or it may be owing to the labour of captives, like the foreign motives in Roman work (see LY 66, 68; WZ 2), or the plait borders unknown at Pompeii, which appear after the Dacian war.

In selecting examples, it seems best to avoid mere intricacy of overloading a basic motive, where no additional idea is added; where such were brought in, it is better to simplify them if too elaborate, as the real motive may be hidden by irrelevant complication. We do not look for hyperboles in an index.

The material subject of a design is only incidental to the quest for motives, whether it be drawn from utility, such as basketry or netting, or from beauty as in plant forms, or from religious symbols as the cross or swastika, or from art and man's device. The scale is immaterial to the nature of the form, and only convenience of size and of detail is followed here. In selection, the earliest examples are always taken, after them the most widely spread, and variants which may be found elsewhere, also any unusually late examples. The mere repetitions of common types in a country are needless for our purpose.

The numbering is designed to allow of the largest amount of expansion without irregularity; thus between 3 and 4 can come 31 to 39.

The first entry in the reference, beneath each drawing, is that of date; if known, in years, it is stated as + for A.D. or — for B.C. If the century alone is known, the middle date is entered. When no definite date is found, a guess has been made from the general circumstances, as being better than nothing, and is marked with a query. The wider divisions are by Egyptian dynasties in Roman numerals, or by the Minoan series, or by the ages of Neolithic, Bronze, and Iron. The nearest equivalents are stated in a table, on the first page of plates.

The second entry is the name of the place, when it is recorded; if obscure, the region is quoted, as the detail can be seen in the original work.

The third entry is that of the source, extracted from over two hundred and fifty works, including many long series. The abbreviations are given in a list. Commoner publications have been preferred, as being easier for verification. Arabic numerals are those of figures, if in a single book, as a translation will retain those numbers; they denote pages, if in a serial. Roman numerals are for volumes (capitals) and plates (small).

It is needless to write obvious conclusions which are seen on looking at the classified examples. Necessary notes of new conclusions and ideas are sometimes put on the plates or, if long, are in print. A plate should explain itself as far as possible, and not be issued in the dignity of silence.

Lantern slides have been made, usually of six or eight subjects together. The negatives are preserved at University College, and whole sets of any one of the 25 classes A to Z can be ordered at a shilling a slide, foreign postage extra.

I have looked forward to doing this work for the last thirty years, and prepared for it. The selection and pencilling are on my own responsibility, and most of the inking in; some inking was done by other hands, and the shields and natural plants are mostly due to Miss Phyllis Gardner's brush work. Any spare space in a plate is left as a blank for making additions.

Those whose purpose is not historical, but artistic, will be aided by the references to the original sources which they require; the sketches here are merely an index.

I hope that every twenty years or so, supplementary plates will be issued by other workers after me, and that a flood of new connections will result from discoveries so much needed in the Middle East. This corpus is a preparation for the co-ordinating of all the new material.

NOTES.

Pls. I-III. *Hero subduing Animals.* The general idea of the A class is that of a controlling deity, which dominates the strongest powers of Nature, represented by lions, bulls, or horses. This symbolism originated in Elam or Iraq, and thence penetrated westward, mainly through Assyrian influence. The Gilgamesh series, AD, is a special form of this idea, but was linked with the rest. The female type is Ishtar, AN, passing into Astarte, AR, mixed with the Mother type of Cybele, AP 8, and the Earth goddess, AP 3, 6. In the West this passes into a deity dominating wolves, AU, or birds, AV, the most intractable creatures.

Pl. IV. *Animals.* The type of two sphinxes, or animals, with a middle column seems to start from Greece, and was continued late there, BA 8. With a middle tree it begins in Egypt, F 1, under Elamite influence; it is early in Iraq, BF 2; from Asia it came into Egypt, BC 8. Pairs of lions without a pillar appear early in Elam, BJ; and sphinxes in the West, BG.

Pl. V. *Animals.* The two snake-headed monsters, BK 2, 4, certainly passed from Sumer to Egypt. The dugong, BM 3, was the figure of Ea the god of wisdom, who rose from the Persian Gulf; it was corrupted in Assyria, as BM 5; thence it passed, under Assyrian influence in the north, to Denmark, M 8. The Glutton head, BN 2, is the main figure in Chinese decoration, where it degraded until formalised as N 4. The twisted snakes type is earliest in Egypt, BP 2, 3, but strangely survives along with rosettes in India, P 5. The form of about 2000 B.C., P 1, has a central staff which brings it nearer to the Caduceus. The two swords with guarded grips are the earliest that we know, P 1.

Pl. VI. *Vase and Animals.* This type originated in a Bacchic group, BT 2, with it a vase and plant became associated, V 2 to 5. Next a vase of fruit appears with birds of any kind, W 2, 4. The peacock was placed in decoration in China before this age, W 3, and first appears in western sculpture, on the porphyry sarcophagus of

Constantia, A.D. 330. At 560 it became usually placed with the vase and plant.

Pl. VII. *Animal Forms.* The triskele appears first about —1500, CB 12; this plain geometrical form, CB 60-75, precedes the development as human legs, CD. A Roman version was the development as dragons' heads, CF. The Chinese dragon seems to be copied from a bird, about —1000, CH 2; it passed under Norse influence, CH 6 (see MQ 3, 6, 84), and became denaturalised, CH 8. The Nautilus passed through various stages since —1800, CN 2. The shell is reduced, the arms formal, by —1300. Later the shell was the main object, with three arms, CO 2, and came down to —500, CO 7. Various other marine animals are difficult to identify.

Pl. VIII. *Octopus.* The naturalistic type, CR 2, of —1800 became regularised by —1600, CR 3, and formal soon after, CR 5. The eight-armed form was revived in the Dipylon ware, CR 8, and seems to have penetrated to the back of China, CR 9, where it is less likely to have been re-invented from the coast. The four-armed type soon arose, about —1400, CT 2, 4, 5. Then the two-armed which lasted to —1300. The period of transfer of the type abroad is thus indicated by the stage of simplifying: to Spain by —1500, to Brittany by perhaps —1200, CU 9. Other forms are of doubtful origin, CX.

Pl. IX. *Naturalistic Plants.* Plant forms are the earliest types of decoration, in France, DM 1, 2, and in Egypt, DM 30-66, at the beginning of prehistoric art. As no magic powers can be supposed to be gained by this variety of species, they warn us against seeing magic intent in the frequent forms of animals; the taste for beauty will produce one as well as the other.

Pl. X. *Lotus.* The lotus was but little varied in Egypt, and it spread mostly from the Assyrian form, DR 4; from this it entered Cyprus and the West, also passing into Scythia, DR 9.

Pls. XI, XII. *Lily.* The lily was adopted in Crete about —2000; EA 2, 5. It became formalised by —1400, EC 3 (see FH 1, 2), and lost to nature, EC 7. In Syria it passed to a different type, BC 8, which was fully treated, as a botanical exposition at Amarna, in —1370. There the parts were clearly set out, ED 2, the pistils (marked P), the anthers (A), the calyx (C), and the spathe with a withered tip (S). These parts continued to be distinguished when the form was borrowed in other lands, down to the Hittite form, EK 7. At this stage it underwent a formalising by the Assyrians, who did not understand it, EM 3, which may be called the bowl type. This went through western stages till it became ES 4, 5, 6, and then grew into a third form, ET 2, 3. Then this ran through a thousand years of classical varieties until it disappeared as EY 7, 8, 9. A detailed account of the development was issued in *Ancient Egypt,* 1929, p. 65.

Pl. XIII. *Palmetto.* The palmetto was brought into Egypt by 2800 B.C., FA 1, and *Emblems* 20, pl. LXXXV. It was greatly developed in Assyria, inserted in volute capitals, FB 2, 4, 5, 6, and adapted to running borders, FC. The Greek types combine the acanthus leaf, FD, with the lotus standing on a degraded form of the lily, FD 5, three subjects in one. Pl. XV. *Formal Flowers.* The fleur-de-lis form is in Japan, FG 3, almost as early as among the Franks, see QK 4. It did not enter Italy in decoration till the Papal Alliance with the Franks against the Lombards in +776, and probably vanished from architecture after Charlemagne. The development of the lily with curled and spiral petals, FH 1, 2, is important for dating this form to 1500 B.C., when it was removed on the way to Britain, 23, 56. Pl. XVIII. The foliage forms seem to pass from acanthus to wild geranium in FU 3, 4. The development of foliage, FV 6, 7, in +800, was growing into a skirl in +750, FV 1, and +825, FV 3, and became disconnected from the branch by +840, FV 8.

Pl. XIX. *Arabesques.* These start in —300, developing a bract at the fork of a branch, GB 12, into a calix form, GB 16, 2. In the Praetextatus catacomb, +180, there was a real reversion to Nature, unique in such work, GB 4, 5. The arabesque became standardised for all apse mosaics of the IV-XII centuries. The Dacian form in GB 9 may have started the Chinese Han type, GC 3 to 8. Pl. XX. *Syrian.* Another strong design was the Syrian vine border, GE 2, 3, which grew into the fine school of the IInd century, GE 7, 8. This was taken up by Rome, GE 5, where it is found by A.D. 130, and passed thus in the Ist century to the Lower Rhine, GE 4, 6. There naturalised, it was carried by the Anglian invasion into England, and it is found upon the Northumbrian crosses, GG 2, 3, 4. The strength of the northern connection appears by the type of the natural interlacing of +750, as seen at Otley, being copied unnaturally in Russia by +1234. With this design in use on the Lower Rhine, there is no need to look to Syrian monks as bringing it to the Anglians.

6

Pl. XXI. *Symmetric*. The translation of formal plant design, GJ 3, 4, to Persia, GJ 5, and China, GJ 6, is probably due to Roman influence. But the Han style, GK 5, must be due to Assyro-Persian influence earlier, as in GK 4, which entered Russia. Pl. XXII. *Foliage Borders*. For the Persian affinity of the Moselle work, GQ 6, and pl. LXXXVI, 70, 83, and LN 71, 75, see Notes LXXXVI.

Pl. XXV. *Rosettes*. The pattern on this Pompeian potter's stamp, HC 2, so closely resembled the Egyptian rosette, HC 3, as to suggest that a piece of old Egyptian design had been brought over in a grain ship to Puteoli, and copied.

Pl. XXVII. *Inanimate*. The hills with plants and flowers, JB 1-7, are an interesting development of scenery in 1400 B.C. The radiate pattern, JE 6, is an extraordinary union of 7 and 13 points. Pl. XXVIII. *Radiate*. The most glorious radiate form is the sun on JQ 6, a yellow disc, with red centre, shining yellow rays and spangles of light on a blue ground.

Pl. XXIX. *Spirals*. The spiral begins before the Neolithic age in the Pyrenees, at the Azilian period, LA 8, LB 6, 10. Perhaps of the same age is that in Egypt of the prehistoric (Amratian) period, LA 13, which suggests a coil of thorny climbing plant, see LXXXV, 32, 33. On the neolithic Danubian pottery, the crossing bands on the spiral suggest that it represented a bundle of grass stems, tied at intervals to make it stiff for construction, LA 26, 28. In either case, it was of flexible vegetable origin, before it became formalised. The full grasp of it was in the aenolithic, with the noble types, LA 58, 63. The S spiral was as early as the whorl, LB 6, 10. Pl. XXX. *The Looped S S* is also aenolithic, LC 16, 18, 20.

Pl. XXXI. *S Continuous*. The multiple band was favoured in Russia and Scandinavia, LC 60, 68, 70, 74, 94, 95, 96: while the spotted band belongs to the south, LC 62, 64, 66; LM 2. In Egypt, the circular spiral, C 86, 87, is of the XI and early XII dynasty, the oval, C 88, 89, is later in the XII, but was started in Ur at an earlier date, LJ 5; it was secondary in Egypt. The S with two sprigs, LD 14, or flowers, D 41, 28, 49, 56, began in —2500, and extended to —1500, LD 56. It was carried west and modified at New Grange, dated on the Irish side between —2000 and —1500. This accords with the Cretan dating. Pl. XXXII. *Band*. The band winding round centres, LE 3, similarly passed to the west and reached Denmark, LE 7, 9, in the same age,

LM 11. Pl. XXXIV. *The C Spiral* begins with LM 19, and seems to rise later than the S form. It is the earliest in Egyptian history, or M 7, about —3400. Pl. XXXVII. *Late Forms*. Spirals became fragmentary in Scythia and the north, LQ. A peculiar decoration with parallel lines of curve, LR, spread from south Russia, just reached Mykenae about 1600, but was otherwise all northern, and spread to China. R 9 and 95 are examples of false spirals, merely circles.

Pls. XXXVIII, XXXIX. *British*. The C spiral was settled in the British Isles, and the form of it, united with the lily with curved petals (extracted at the side of LS 56), comes from the flower, FH 1, 2, of —1500. The trumpet spiral was started in Crete, LV 4, about —1500 or earlier; it had passed to Britain by about +100, LX 4, and was eagerly developed later in Britain, LX 5, 7, and Ireland, LX 8, 9. The use in Britain was long before the period of Irish missions, and its arrival must have been in the Bronze Age, before it vanished from the south, probably about —1500 when other spiral patterns were transmitted. These spirals were here a thousand years before the Celts, who adopted what they found here already. The inflated style, LW, may be due to Celtic taste in each case, as it does not appear before that people. How usual spirals were for common purposes is seen in LX 98, 99, on objects in use.

Pl. XL. *Spiral Blobs*. The blob form, LY belongs to the North, a later growth of the bulbous, LV, and inflated, LW. It entirely disappeared after the Roman age, but revived by racial taste under Louis Quinze, LY 96, and infected the jewellery and furniture of that time. It appears on Roman lamps, Y 67, 68, probably due to the employment of the Gaulish captives of Caesar in the Roman potteries. The joining of spirals with a circle (often with double centres) in Britain is pre-Roman, LZ; then of Roman age in LX 4, and it continued into the Lindisfarne work, LX 5.

Pl. XLVI. *Interlacing Designs* belong originally to Norway, MN 2, 3; thence they were brought by the Anglian invasion into north England, N 4, 5, 54, 6, 66. They do not appear in Ireland till a later date, and they have no relation to the Celts, as plaits enter the British Isles a thousand years later than the Celts. Similar angular interlacing, as in rush work, entered Italy with the Lombards, and not earlier (MN 7, 73, 76, 79). It was combined with circular curves, partly by +700, MN 54, and completely by +825, MO 2. From Milan, O 4, +880, it passed to Ireland +924. It continued in more complex forms in Italy till +1132, MO 8. It is distinguished from interlacing of the Goths, for that was not angular, but curved, as in osier work, see MH 65, 68, 69. The origin of all such interlacing is probably for the screens used to subdivide tents.

Pl. XLVII. *Animal Interlacing.* Interlacing was elaborated by the Norse with animal figures and dragons, MP. The complex dragon plaiting, MQ 8 (one animal shaded to show the form), gave rise to a figure of 8 pattern, MQ 84. Wire work was developed in the north, MU 2 to 5, by +680, and copied after the Norse invasion of Ireland, MU 7, B, of +850 onward. Wire threading on a chain was also imitated, MR 4.

Pl. L. The divisions of a circle are by 4 in Egypt and early Crete, where compass-struck patterns were unknown; but by 6 in Assyria, Syria, Greece and Italy, owing to facility of division by compasses. Pls. LI, LII. *The Skirl* seems to be intended to indicate circular motion, as in PT 9, the drawing of a chariot wheel.

Pls. LIII, LIV. *Shields.* The shields of northern races yield much of the decoration which has otherwise all perished in their woodwork. The Daci, on the column of Trajan, used vegetative forms, QC, D, and the crescent QE. Torques were worn by Daci, QF, and by Celts, QG; one was on the left arm, as in the story of Tarpeia, and two or four for higher ranks. On the column of Aurelius, the enemy in chain armour were the Marcomanni, as such armour was used in Holstein, QH. The Quadi used scale armour of horn (Ammianus), and this identifies the type, QK 1. The fleur-de-lis, K 4, is probably of the Franci, who were in the war of A.D. 417. The shields, QR 2, 3, 4, may be of Roman legions. The circular shield belonged to Greece and Gaul, QT, V. The Scythian type is identified by QX 2, but became so fashionable in art, that it is hard to draw conclusions from its presence in Gaul, X 5, and Etruria, X 6, 7. For the signs on Scottish gravestones, which appear to be shields and broken spears, see Pl. LXXXVII: as this origin has not yet been discussed, they are left in the miscellaneous class.

Pl. LV. *Band of Balls.* This pattern seems poor as a design, but it was very popular in the north. It touched the south at Mykenae, RN 4, and north Italy under the Lombards, RP 84, Q 4, RR 1, 2, 4, 5, 6, but never rooted there. It entered England, Q 2, 3, with the Jutes, and is found rarely on early fonts. Pl. LVI. *Architecture.* A surprising feature, which has been overlooked, is the early use of the arch. In the neolithic age in Germany there were pillars and arches, RX 2, apparently of brickwork, with stone capitals. In Cappadocia very early arches are figured, RX 3; and in Mykenae by —1700 there were actually pointed arches, RX 4. After these, it seems likely that the later figures, X 5, 6, 7 were also of arched buildings. The spiral column, which was early in Mykenae, BC 6, was in Italy by —500, RY 3, and in India by +200, Y 5.

Pl. LVII. *The Cross* was an early emblem, in Susa by about —3000, and in India, SA 4, distinguished by a double border, SA 1 to 4. This gives reason for regarding the sign in Egypt at the same time, A 6, 7, as being an emblem, and not merely a mechanical piece of line-work. It was equally known between these two countries, in Cilicia and Aleppo, A 8, 9. The more ornate barred ends, B 5 were added not later than —2000. The sign is also bordered in Egypt, C 7, and Melos, C 8. By —2600 the cross began to be elaborated in Crete, SD, and D 2 is an astonishingly early example, not far from the primitive figure, A 2. It fell into a coarser treatment on the mainland, SE. This pure equilateral form, without any ornament, SF 4, was that in the shrine at Knossos, dating about 2300 B.C., and is exactly the same as the well-known Greek cross of Christian times. It was also used in the north, by the example F 3, from Laibach. It was adapted to woven stuff for clothing, SF 7, 8, and by —1400 in a fanciful form, G 7, 8, it was probably made in Crete, and imported to Egypt for hangings. After that, it became degraded, SJ. In Assyria, SK 5 to 9, the terminals were emphasized, and copied thus in the north, SK 2.

Pl. LIX. *Christian Age.* On reaching Christian times, it is clear that the pagan forms were retained, M 3 continued as N 1, 12; M 1, continued as N 15; N 4 continued as N 45. None of the pagan ornate forms were used religiously till the Vth century, A.D. (O9,O97). Pl. LX. In the Christian monuments, the XP monogram begins in +331, and lasts till +470. The variant with the P made with Horus' lock of hair, begins +440, and continued to +560, but is common in Egypt later. The plain figure of the cross first appears in +380, and the jewelled cross in +425. The expanded terminals begin about +450. The Arian cross has discs at the terminals, SX 1, 12. The adored cross at Palenque, in Central America, has terminals of the type of +600. Such a cross may well have been taken by the Nestorian mission in +638

8

to China, and within the next five centuries there may have been Chinese communication with America.

A very important movement was the reforming activity of Leo the Isaurian, who tried to bring the Byzantine empire and law into a more modern condition. Part of the change was the iconoclast movement in A.D. 730, to which we must ascribe the removal of the arms from the great crosses at Constantinople, on the west doors of Hagia Sofia; and this reformation was reflected in 820, when the Archbishop of Turin abolished crosses and images in his diocese. To the same movement is due the erasure of the cross arms at the church of S. Prassede in Rome, SY 6. In 830 the cross received the addition of a second bar higher up; this short cross-piece may have represented the label, INRI; SZ 2, 6.

Pl. LXIII. *Triangle.* Among triangles should be noticed the peculiar half rhombs, TR 7, 8, 9. On the last named the circles contain two small circles, as in late Celtic work elsewhere, LX 1, 4, 5; Z 4, 5, 6. Some meaning may have been attached to the sign. The curious type of the triangle with a disc on the point is as early as —1100 (TS 1), and appears again at —400 (TS 56). The main example of it on the tomb of Theodoric, TS 6, is too late in date to give a clue to understanding it. Rhombs subdivided were the favourite type about —600 (TZ).

Pl. LXVI. *Textiles.* Among weaving patterns, there is a large variety copied in the brickwork of mediaeval Iraq, UP. The reason for this is that matting is often placed over mud brick walls to preserve them from weather, and so the patterns of matting were naturally associated with such building. The net-work patterns, UN, in Britain are copied from the string nets in which pots were carried, as they were in Egypt. Hanging drapery, UR, was often in use on walls, and is one of the commonest painted subjects. The great example of imitation is in the marble stripes lining the cathedral of Monreale, marked out by the red borders of each width represented, and striped marble was selected for the apse, which simulated hangings.

Pls. LXIX, LXX. *The Swastika* is more commonly pointing backward (V; E, F, G), than forward (V; A, B). The groups here are of the simple form, then with one extra bend, and others up to 5 bends. Each group is arranged geographically from west to east, to show the distribution. The eastern is the earlier source. On the Indian form, see *Ancient Egypt*, 1922, 56.

Pl. LXXI. *Grooves and Steps.* The origin of the "strigil" pattern, WB 6, on Roman sarcophagi is traced back here to wide fluting, W, A and B. The step pattern, W, G to K, is purely northern, and only touches the Mediterranean at one corner. It is very persistent, and is now in general use from Scotland to China. It took possession of the gold and garnet work, which originally (WJ 2), was free from it, and ruled all the Jutish and Saxon jewellery work in England, WK 2, 3. Pls. LXXIII-IV. *Mosaics* are classed by the obliquity of the angles formed, 1:1 up to 1:3. The long hexagon embroidery in Assyria, Z 6, is evidently derived from two hexagons, one above the other, as in Z 5. The Solomon's Seal pattern, WZ 2 was probably due to Jewish captives employed.

Pl. LXXV. *Key.* The simple key patterns abound in Italy, the more interesting are the reciprocal forms, where the inter-spaces are of the same form as the solid between them, as in XA 8, and XD. The maze pattern XE 2 is the oldest known. XE 6 is not perfect, as the upper left-hand quarter does not open. Pl. LXXX. *Squares.* The expanded cross of Hartlepool, YN 7, is derived from the Ravenna type, N 5, and that obviously came from an Etruscan origin, N 4. Pl. LXXXII. The curious pattern YW 5 seems to have been copied from a grating above a doorway. The squares of varied content, YY and YZ, show what the Celt did before he acquired the spiral or interlaced forms.

Pl. LXXXIII. *The Metopic* series, ZA to E, was developed to separate squares of design around vases. In this form it precedes by a thousand years the architectural use of parallel lines between metopic groups. There is no meaning in grooving the ends of the roof beams in a building; but when that device of parallel lines to separate groups was well fixed in vase painting, it naturally was transferred to a similar duty in architecture.

Pl. LXXXV. *Emblems.* Over the head of Hittite deities is placed the sign 10 A, B, C, 11, which is recognised as the sign of divinity. It may represent a double shrine of the Mother and Son deities. A modification of this, 12, is placed beneath each of five divine figures, on a gold ring from Tiryns. The same is developed as 15 at Knossos, and this passed on to the types 16, 18 and 19; the last-named still retains the double bar of 10 A to C. Whether the Cretans recognised the original sense is quite unknown; apparently, it is merely used as ornament. Another emblem is that of the Hittite royal mark, which is found on pottery and elsewhere, 21-2-3. It appears as an amulet at Amarna, 27; also as a mould for making such amulets, No. 28; this suggests that the Egyptians traded pendants or amulets with the Hittites. A gold amulet of this type is also known, Z 9.

On the dress of the Kefti people, about the north-east of the Mediterranean, in 1600 B.C., there is placed an emblem, 36; this belonged to a previous age, as examples occur in Egypt at 2700 B.C., 32, 33; we cannot say from where they were introduced. In Asia it passed to Kashgar (37), to a reliquary of Persian (?) sources (38), and up to Lithuania, 39.

Pl. LXXXVI. Some groups are hardly assignable to any of the main classes. Fresh connections may appear in future. The wave group, 61-69, links on to some in the spiral group, LP 37, 56, of the same period and regions: but the wave forms could not all go among spirals; in order to separate these classes, far earlier examples would be needed. The strange divergent droops, 70 to 79, are unexplained: in 75 they seem to show a structure which recalls Persian or Central Asian design. The Persian affinity of 70 and 83 is puzzling in the Franco-German region; the rest of the group is in GQ 6, 7, and LN 71. In 83 the flower at the top, the droops on each side, the two commas below, and the droops at the base, are all of the fashion of Persian work, as on the dress of Khusrau, 84. Was it due to a stray party from Xerxes' expedition at 480 B.C., lost in Thrace, and pushing west to the Rhine? Their superior civilisation might well take a lead in that region. In Hagia Sofia, 85, the middle figure is almost Turkish, and is duplicated in the very foreign group in Britain, 82. Below in group 91 to 95 is the series of boss designs from China; this is an Asiatic idea which crops up in the large oval boss from the Caucasus, WJ 8, and in Asiatic-Gothic elsewhere.

Pl. LXXXVII. The Scottish emblems on tombstones have been supposed to represent a fibula and pin; but no pin could have a widening at each end, nor be bent. It seems rather that the group represents some form of shield reversed, and the broken spear, of a warrior. Such a long, round-ended, shield as QZ 3, 4 appears QP 4, 6, and accords with the style of Celtic shields, as seen in the example from the Thames, QZ, 46. The lunate form, QZ 6 may be the Scythian shield, QX, QY; the deeper form QZ 5 is parallel to the deeper forms QX 8, 9. The squared forms QZ 66-77 may be a square basket-work breastplate,

like the square front and back pieces on Gaulish figures at Marseilles. In the sides are circular hollows to allow freedom for the arms and, below, it descends in two cuisses over the thighs. The spear points remain in Z 2, 3, 6, 62, 64, 66. The whole idea seems to have been originally the reversing of the shield, laid longways or upside down, and the breaking of the spear, like the heralds breaking their wands at a funeral, as symbols of the end of the career. On one stone a helmet is also figured, see ACM 99. This custom would have arisen in the Bronze Age, and in the post-Christian period of these monuments the originals were probably forgotten, more or less, and the forms were confused. It may be mentioned that the animal on these tombstones, sometimes called an elephant, is probably a walrus.

Pl. LXXXVIII contains mysterious forms which may some day find a place in the series when we have much more material before us.

To sum up some of the results that we can already gain from this study: there is the great influence of Assyria on the North, in Hungary (SK 2, 5) on the Lower Dnieper (DR 9, FA 9, GK 4, 5), and extending to Denmark (BM 8); there is the movement at 1500 B.C. from Crete and Mykenae to Britain, which was probably by the Atlantic, and not from Northern lands where such designs are unknown (FH 1=LS 56, LD 56=LD 97, LE 3=LE 7, 9, LN 63=LN 67, CU 3=CU 9); there is the Syrian vine copied on the Lower Rhine, and thence brought to Northumbria by the Anglians; there is the interlaced work coming from Norway, brought by the Anglians to England, and by the Danes to Ireland; there is the Han style in China due to Assyro-Persian work; there is the Hittite divine emblem planted in Crete, and the royal emblem in Egypt; and there is the rise of arched brickwork in neolithic Germany, in Cappadocia, and with pointed arches in Mykenae. Lastly, there is a strong evidence of a wandering body from the army of Xerxes reaching the Lower Rhine.

These are some of the more definite conclusions which may already be drawn from a study of these decorative patterns; when more material is available one may expect to find many more links in the earlier ages. From these we shall view the past as a network of civilisations, peculiar to each land, and interacting on each other. We may then discriminate the original source of each of the devices which belonged to different areas before they were spread by intercourse.

ABBREVIATIONS.

A	Archaeologia	53
AA	Archiv für Anthrop.	1
AAF	Aspelin, Antiq. Nord. Finn	9
AAS	Aberg, Anglo-Saxons	20
ABA	Abercromby, Bronze Age	25
ABS	Ann. Brit. Sch. Athens	55
ACA	Andrae, Ceramics of Ashur	3
ACM	R. Allen Early Christian Mons.	8
ACWA	Ayrton, C. and W., Abydos 1904	1
A-E	Ancient Egypt	61
AFW	Aberg, Franken, West-Goten	25
AGL	Aberg, Goten, Langobarden	23
AGO	Armstrong, Gold Ornaments	1
AJA	American Jour. Archaeology	8
AM	Athenische Mittheilungen	4
AN	L'Anthropologie	5
ANT.R	Antiquarium, Rome	2
AO	Alt Orient	1
AS	Andrae-Schäfer	1
AV	Arne, Necropole Vendel	12
AZ	Arch. Zeitung, Berlin	8
BAB	Boye, Age Bronze, Danemarc	2
BAE	Baldwin Brown, Arts Early England	16
BAK	Bossert, Alt Kreta	12
BAMI	Burgess, Anc. Mons., India	2
BAS	Blavignac, Archit. Sacrée	16
BAZ	Bull. Soc. Scien. Azerbijan	3
BC	Bertrand & Reinach, Celtes du Po	42
BCA	Boerschmann, Chines. Archit.	9
BEO	Brønsted, Early English Ornament	16
BGG	Bulleid & Gray, Glastonbury	28
BHG	Boyd & Hawes, Gournia	4
BIS	Banks, Bismiya	1
BK	Blegen, Korakou	15
BL	Brunton, Lahun I	1
BLM	Blackman, Meir	1
BM	British Museum	5
BMB	Boston Mus., Bulletin	2
BMCE	Brit. Mus. Cat., Early Iron Age	15
BME	Bliss-Macalister, Excavations	1
BMJ	Brit. Mus. Cat., Jewellery	1
BN	Botta, Ninève	4
BNS	Butler, North Syria	6
BP	Briggs, Pompeian Decoration	4
BQB	Brunton, Qau and Badari	3
BRG	Babelon, Monnaies Repub., Rome	3
BSA	Butler, Syrian Anc. Architecture	13
BU	Bell, Ukhaidir	4
BZ	Blegen, Zygouries	5
CA	Childe, G., Aryans	6
CAB	Chantré, Age du Bronze	1
CAC	Chifletius Anastasis Childerici	2
CAF	Chantré Prem. Age du Fer	8
CAI	Cattaneo, Archit. in Italy	4
CAO	Contenau, Archéol. Orientale	1
CB	Carabellesi, Bari	1
CC	Chantré, Caucase, I, II, III	18
CCO	Crawford, Carved Ornament, Irish	43
CD	Childe, Dawn Europ. Civilization	23
CDA	Capart, Débuts de l'Art, Egypte	2
CDURA	Cumont, Doura	1
CDP	Childe, Danube in Prehistory	13
CIP	Cohn, Indisches Plastik	8
CMC	Chantré, Miss. Cappadoce	2
CNG	Coffey, New Grange	6
CT	Cichorius, Traianus Säule	7
DA	Ducate, Arte	5
DCD	Delbrueck, Consular Diptychen	12
DCL	Delaporte, Cylindres, Louvre	33
DCO	Delaporte, Cylindres Orientaux	3
DCP	Dussaud, Civil. Préhelléniques	8
DECA	Dalton, Early Christian Art	3
DF	Déchellete, Age du Fer	16
DF2	Déchellete, Second Age du Fer	26
DP	Délégation en Perse	5
EDE	Engelhardt, Denmark, Early Iron Age	4
EG	Espérandieu, Gaule Romaine	60
EH	Engelbach, Harageh	1
EM	Ernest Mackay, correspondence	14
EN	Excavaciones Numancia, 1912	13

EPH	Ephemeris, Athens	.	.	.	.	1
EPM	Evans, Palace of Minos, I, II	.	.	.	78
EPT	Evans, Prehistoric Tombs	.	.	.	3
ESA	Einstein, Scultura Africana	.	.	.	2
ESB	Evans, Shaft Graves, Beehive Tombs	.	1
ESM	Evans, Scripta Minoa	.	.	.	.	2
ETP	Evans, Tree and Pillar Cult	.	.	.	1
FCL	Fellows, Lycian Coins	.	.	.	.	5
FG	Furtwängler, Gemmen	.	.	.	.	1
FLM	Furtwängler & Loescheke, Myken. Vasen	.	57
FLT	Furtwängler & Loescheke, Thongefässe	.	2
FMP	Fowler, W., Mosaic Pavements	.	.	1
FNZ	Faenza (Journal)	.	.	.	.	1
FP	Flinders Petrie copy	.	.	.	39
FRV	Furtwängler & Reichold, Vasen	.	.	1
FV	Falchi, Vetulonia	.	.	.	.	1
GA	Gusman, Art décoratif, Rome	.	.	14
GBA	Gervasio, Bronzi Arcaichi	.	.	.	23
GC	Gruneisen, Arte Copte	.	.	.	16
GCC	Genouillac, Céramique Cappadoce	.	28
GCK	Gluck, Christliche Kunst	.	.	.	6
GEC	George, W. S., Church of St. Eirene	.	2
GM	Germania Romana	.	.	.	.	2
GN	Gardner, E., Naukratis II	.	.	.	2
H	Hill, B. M. Catalogues of Coins	.	.	5
HAR	Halle, Arte Russa antica	.	.	.	2
HBK	Hoernes, Urges. Bildenden Kunst	.	.	14
HEE	Hogarth, Excavations at Ephesus	.	.	8
HF	Holland, L. A., The Faliscans	.	.	4
HFD	Hersfeld, Fels Denkmal Irans	.	.	3
HH	Hogarth, Hittite Seals	.	.	.	8
HOC	Hall, H. R., Oldest Civil. Greece	.	.	1
HS	Hall, E. H., Sphungaras	.	.	.	1
HSI	Herbert, Schools of Illuminating	.	.	1
HSM	Hamada, Sumitomo Mirrors	.	.	9
HU	Hoernes, Urgeschichte Menschen	.	.	17
HW	Hayes Ward, Seal Cylinders	.	.	26
HWU	Hall & Woolley, Al Ubaid	.	.	.	8
ILN	Illustrated London News	.	.	.	2
JDE	Jéquier, Décoration Egyptien	.	.	10
JHK	Jack & Hayter, Kenchester	.	.	.	2
JHS	Journal of Hellenic Studies	.	.	28
JI	Jahrb. Inst. Deut. Archäol.	.	.	18
JOAI	Jahrb. Oester. Arch. Inst.	.	.	9
JRS	Journal of Roman Studies	.	.	.	7
JSA	Janssen & Savignac, Miss. Arabie	.	2
JSH	Joyce, P. W., Social History, Ireland	.	2
KB	Kunstgeschichte in Bildern	.	.	51
KM	Kircherian Museum	.	.	.	21
KSA	King, Hist. Sumer and Akkad	.	.	1
KT	Koch, Dachterrakotten Campanien	.	40
KUE	Körte, Rel. Urne Etrusche	.	.	2
KWE	Koldeway, Wieder Ersteh. Babylon	.	2
LA	Lindenschmidt, Alterthümer	.	.	13
LAM	Lacroix, Arts du Moyen Age	.	.	1
LEYDEN, Monuments, Catalogue		.	.	.	1
LIOY	Abitazione Lacustre Fimon	.	.	1
LK	Lübke	.	.	.	.	.	3
LN	Layard, Monuments of Nineveh	.	12
LOUVRE Museum Catalogue		.	.	.	1
LP	Lefebvre, Tombeau Petosiris	.	.	2
LV	Lindqvist, Vendel Kulturens	.	.	1
LW	Lysons, Woodchester	.	.	.	4
MA	Monumenti Antichi	.	.	.	167
MAA	Mem. Amer. Acad., Rome	.	.	13
MADP	de Morgan, Age de Pierre	.	.	1
MAE	Munsterberg, Art Extrême Orient	.	5
MAIA	Mitt. Arch. Inst. Athenische	.	25
MAK	Montelius, Alter. Kulturperioden	.	31
MAM	Micali, Antichi Monumenti	.	.	00
MANX	Kermode, Manx Crosses	.	.	3
MAP	Meyer, Apulien	.	.	.	58
MBH	Wiss. Mitt. Bosnien Herzogovina	.	23
MC	Montelius, Vorklass. Chronol. Italien	7
MCA	de Morgan, Caucase	.	.	.	1
MCH	Macdonald, Cat., Hunterian	.	.	2
MCS	Montelius, Civilization, Sweden	.	5
MF	Mainz, Festschrift Lindenschmidt	.	3
MG	Museo Gregoriano	.	.	.	2
MGA	Mosaïques, Gaule et l'Afrique	.	4
MGP	Montelius Grèce Préclassique	.	11
MI	,, Prim. Civilis. Ital.	.	.	113
MIA	Museo Italiano di Antichità	.	.	2
MKE	Mühlestein, Kunst der Etrusker	.	2
MLG	Miller, Lindisfarne Gospels	.	.	6
MLW	Munro, Lake Dwellings	.	.	2
MMA	Minto, Marsiliana d'Albegna	.	1
MOD	Müller & Oesterley, Denkmäler	.	5
MON. DIV. Monuments Divers, Cairo		.	1
MP	Monuments Piot	.	.	.	3
MPG	Mosso, Palaces of Crete	.	.	6
MPO	de Morgan, Préhistoire Orientale	.	5
MS	Metz, Frühkretischen Siegel	.	32
MSAC	Maraghiannis & Seager, Ant. Cret.	.	4
MSE	Murray Ainslie, Symbolism	.	.	7
MSG	Minns, Scythians and Greeks	.	5
NAA	Nielsen, Altarabische Kultur	.	2
NB	Northcote & Brownlow, Roma Sotteranea	.	4
NF	Nordiska Fortidsminder	.	.	5
NS	Notizie degli Scavi	.	.	.	33
NSO	Nerman, Skandinav. Ostbaltikum	.	5
ODE	Oulié, Décoration Egéenne	.	.	2
OLYMPIA		.	.	.	.	1
OTP	Odoresco, Trésor de Petroassa	.	4
PA	Petrie, Amarna	.	.	.	33
PAB	,, Abydos, I, II	.	.	.	1

CLASSES AND FAMILIES OF ARRANGEMENT.

			No.	Plate.
A		**Hero and Lions, Ishtar.**		
B	Elamite, Egyptian	. .	2	I
D	Gilgamesh . . .	.	3	
F	Persia to Italy .	.	7	
H	Hero and bulls, horses, ostriches . . .	.	5	II
J	Italian . . .	.	4	
K	Heads . . .	.	2	
N	Ishtar . . .	.	4	
P	Earth goddess, Cybele	.	3	
R	Astarte and lions	.	12	III
S	Astarte and animals	.	3	
U	Goddess and wolves	.	2	
V	Goddess and swans	.	9	
B		**Sphinxes and Animals.**		
A	Sphinxes and pillar	.	4	IV
C	Animals and pillar or plant	.	5	
F	Animals and tree	.	7	
G	Pair of sphinxes .	.	4	
J	Pair of lions .	.	3	
K	Pair of monsters	.	3	V
M	Dugong . . .	.	3	
N	Sloth head . .	.	4	
O	Stags, cats . .	.	2	
P	Serpents entwined, insects	.	10	
Q	Pair of swans .	.	4	
T	Vase and animals	.	5	VI
V	Vase and plant	.	5	
W	Vase and birds .	.	9	
C		**Triskele, dragons, nautilus.**		
B,C	Triskele . . .	.	17	VII
D	Three legs . .	.	6	
F	Dragon heads .	.	4	
H	Chinese dragon .	.	4	
J	Pair of dolphins .	.	2	
N	Nautilus . . .	.	9	
O	Nautilus shell .	.	3	
P	Loligo, etc. . .	.	8	
R	Octopus, 8 arms	.	8	VIII
S	,, 6 arms	.	1	
T	,, 4 arms	.	4	
U	,, 2 arms	.	7	
X	,, ? .	.	5	
D		**Natural plants.**		
A	Crocus . . .	.	4	IX
C	Pink . . .	.	3	
E		. .	5	
F	Vetch . . .	.	1	

			No.	Plate.
G	Star anemone .	. .	1	
H		. .	7	
J	Lily of the valley	.	1	
K		. .	1	
L	Olive . . .	.	4	
M		. .	19	
N		**Natural plants. Lotus.**		
N	Palm . . .	.	1	X
O	Various . . .	.	6	
P	Lotus, natural .	.	1	
Q	,, grouped .	.	4	
R	,, Assyrian .	.	5	
S	,, Italian .	.	5	
T	,, Greek .	.	1	
U	,, ,, formal	.	1	
W	,, Roman .	.	1	
X	,, artificial .	.	1	
Y	,, borders .	.	3	
Z	,, petals .	.	2	
E		**Lily.**		
A	Natural . . .	.	2	XI
C	Formal . . .	.	5	
D	Egyptian . . .	.	6	
G	,, formal	.	8	
H	Oriental . . .	.	7	
J	Flower group .	.	1	
K	Arborescent .	.	6	
M	Bowl form, Assyrian	.	3	
N	Palmetto, Assyrian	.	1	XII
P	,, Cretan, etc.	.	5	
Q	,, Italian	.	6	
S	Bowl, Italian .	.	8	
T	Fan, Italian .	.	14	
Y	Persian, Indian, Byzantine	.	9	
F		**Palmetto and Formal.**		
A	Egypt, Assyria .	.	8	XIII
B	Compound, as capital	.	7	
C	Repeated border .	.	18	
D	Acanthus . . .	.	9	XIV
E	,, border	.	5	
F	,, debased	.	7	
G	Fleur-de-lis .	.	6	XV
H	Formal flowers .	.	9	
J	,, borders .	.	10	
K	Radiate flower .	.	12	XVI
L	Stem flower .	.	9	
M	Geometric flower .	.	15	
N	Vine border .	.	6	

3064

AB4

B7

D3

S.D.63 HIERAKONPOLIS, QGH, LXXVI
—5000?
EGYPTIAN COPY

HW.159

GILGAMESH

—5000?   GEBELELARAQ   M.P.

ELAMITE WORK IN EGYPT
AT THE CONQUEST S.D.63

F2

PERSIAN CYL. HW,1108

F4

D6

D8

F3

HW.165

CRETE, IDEAN CAVE
OVERHEAD
M.+A.II,i

CORINTH AZ·1884 VIII

—400? DORYLAION
MAIA 1895 I

ASSYRIAN INFLUENCE IN CRETE
GILGAMESH AND THE BULL

F6

F7

F8

NINEVEH L.N.II.64

—500   SEALING MEMPHIS   P.W.M,XXXVI

BRONZE, SABAEAN   N·A·A· 67

F9

H1

H3

BRONZE, PERUGIA,   M.I.252,17

—350 ATHENS, MARBLE THRONE, MAIA,1926,124

—730 NIMRUD   L·N·XLViii

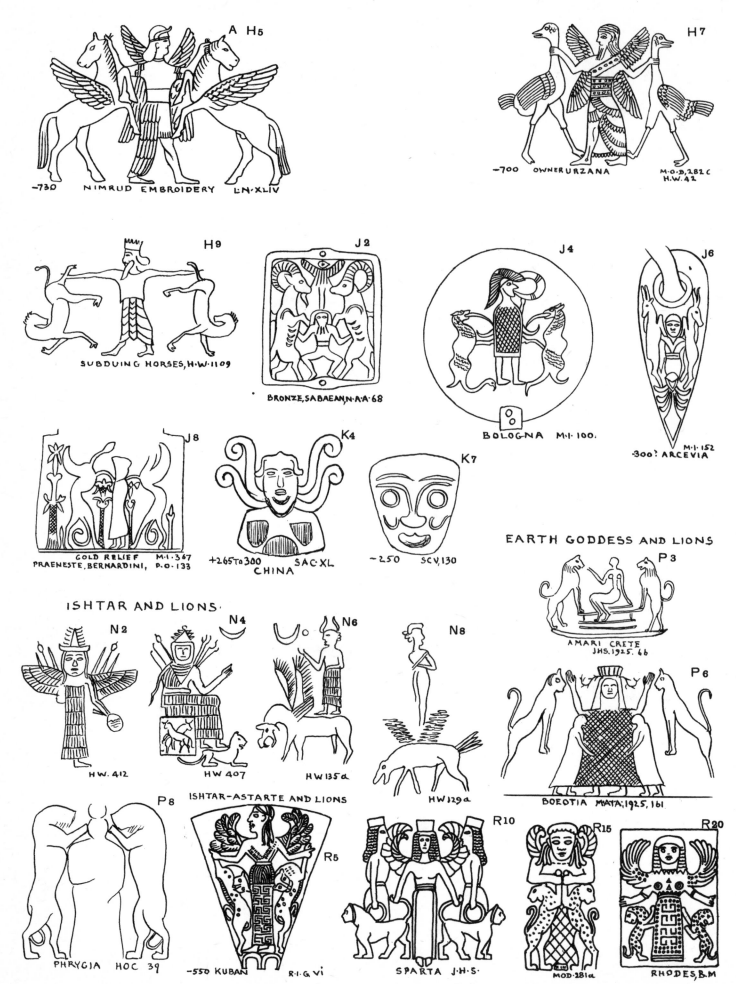

A H5

-730   NIMRUD EMBROIDERY   L·N·XLIV

H7

-700   OWNER URZANA   M·O·D·282C   H.W.42

H9
SUBDUING HORSES, H·W·1109

J2
BRONZE, SABAEAN, N·A·A·68

J4
BOLOGNA   M·I·100.

J6
-300? ARCEVIA   M·I·152

J8
GOLD RELIEF   M·I·367
PRAENESTE, BERNARDINI, P.O·133

K4
+265 TO 300   SAC·XL
CHINA

K7
-250   SCV.130

EARTH GODDESS AND LIONS

P3
AMARI CRETE   JHS.1925. 66

P6
BOEOTIA   MATA: 1925, 161

ISHTAR AND LIONS·

N2
HW. 412

N4
HW 407

N6
HW 135a

N8
HW 129a

P8
PHRYGIA   HOC 39

ISHTAR-ASTARTE AND LIONS

R5
-550 KUBAN   R·I·G·VI

R10
SPARTA   J·H·S.

R15
MOD·281a

R20
RHODES, B.M

AR 25
~550 OLYMPIA, IV, XXXVIII

R 30
~550 KLAZOMENAI

R 35
~800? EPHESOS
P.O.30

R 40
IDAEAN CAVE, CRETE
MIA II T.X
K.B.101

R 45
MOD. 2815

R 50
BERLIN. MAA·I, XVI
granular work.

R 55
CAPUA   K.T. XVI

R 60
~670   CAERE   M.I. 341

S 3
~550 FRANÇOIS VASE F.R.V.

S 5
SYRACUSE
NS 1895 119
IVORY

S 8
~730   CORNETO   R.M.V. 31

U 3
ATHENS   K.B. 116

U 6
~800' VETULONIA, M·I. 178, 16

V 1
IVORY AT HALLE
MAIA 1925 VII

V 2
LM·I· THISBE GOLD RING
JHS 1925 23

V 3
BOEOTIA BOX
JHS 1925 24

V 4
ARKADIA CRETE
MAIA·1926, 59

V 5
MOD 282A

V 6
650? SPARTA
ABS 1907 80

V 7
MAM·LXXV.   MOD.282B

V 8
~750? SPARTA, A·B·S
1907·78

V 9
CAPUA   K.T. XII

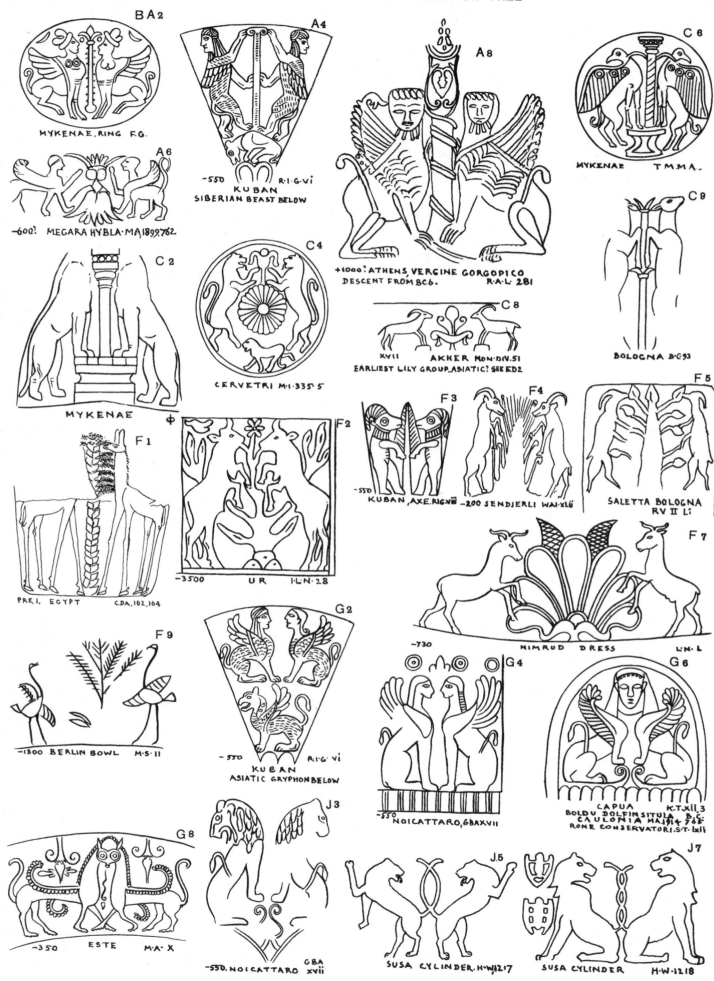

BA2
MYKENAE, RING F.G.

A4
-550   R·I·G·Vi
KUBAN
SIBERIAN BEAST BELOW

A8
+1000? ATHENS, VERGINE GORGOPICO
DESCENT FROM BC6.   R·A·L· 281

C6
MYKENAE   T·M·M·A·

A6
-600? MEGARA HYBLA MA 1899.762

C2
MYKENAE

C4
CERVETRI M·I·335·5

C8
XVII   AKKER MON·DIV·51
EARLIEST LILY GROUP, ASIATIC? SEE ED2

C9
BOLOGNA B·G·93

F1
PRE.I. EGYPT   CDA,162,164

F2
-3500   UR   I·L·N·28

F3
-550
KUBAN, AXE. RIG·Viii

F4
-200 SENDJERLI WAI·XLii

F5
SALETTA BOLOGNA
RV II Li

F7
-730   NIMRUD DRESS   L·N·L

F9
-1300 BERLIN BOWL   M·S·II

G2
-550   R·I·G· Vi
KUBAN
ASIATIC GRYPHON BELOW

G4
-550 NOICATTARO, G·B·A XVII

G6
CAPUA   K.T.Xii.3
BOLDU DOLFIN SITULA   B·C·
CAULONIA MA 1914 768
ROME CONSERVATORI.ST.lxii

G8
-350   ESTE   M·A·X

J3
-550. NOICATTARO   G·B·A
XVii

J.5
SUSA CYLINDER. H·W·1217

J7
SUSA CYLINDER   H·W·1218

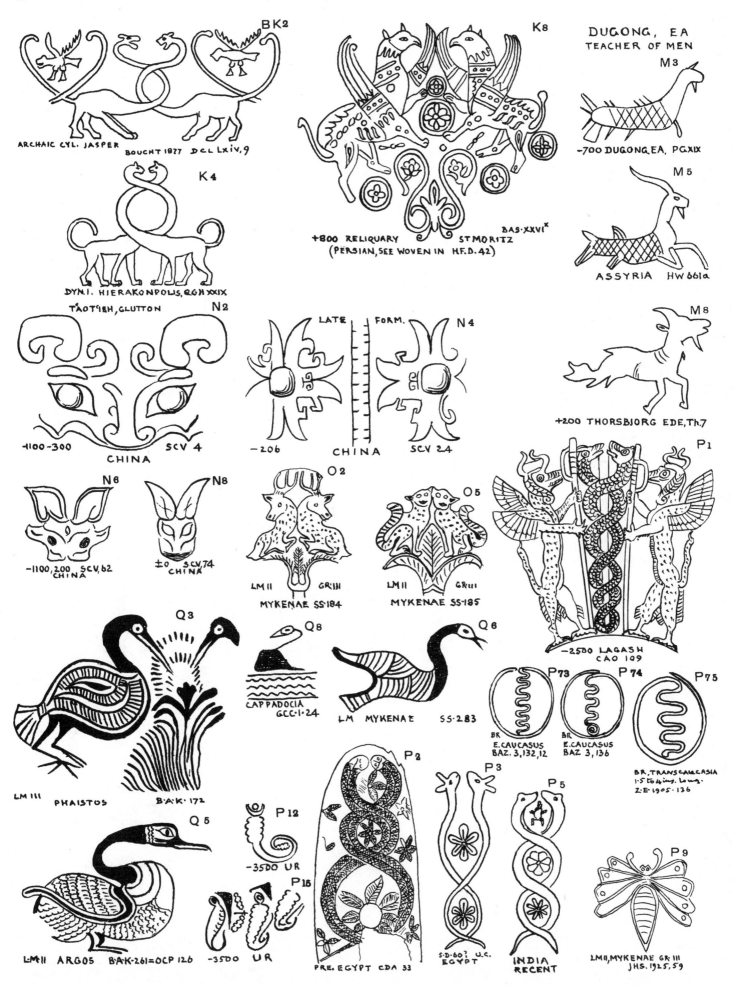

BK2
ARCHAIC CYL. JASPER
BOUCHT 1877 DCL LXIV, 9

K4
DYN. I. HIERAKONPOLIS, QGH XXIX

K8

+800 RELIQUARY   ST MORITZ
(PERSIAN, SEE WOVEN IN H.F.D. 42)
BAS. XXVI

DUGONG, EA
TEACHER OF MEN
M3
-700 DUGONG, EA, PG XIX

M5
ASSYRIA   HW 661a

TÁOT'IEH, GLUTTON   N2
-1100-300   SCV 4
CHINA

LATE   FORM.   N4
-206   CHINA   SCV 24

M8
+200 THORSBJORG EDE, Th.7

N6
-1100, 200   SCV, 62
CHINA

N8
±0   SCV, 74
CHINA

O2
LM II   GR. III
MYKENAE SS·184

O5
LM II   GR. III
MYKENAE SS·185

P1
-2500 LAGASH
CAO 109

Q3
LM III   PHAISTOS   B·A·K· 172

Q8
CAPPADOCIA
GCC·1·24

Q6
LM MYKENAE   SS·2·83

P73   P74   P75
BR   BR
E. CAUCASUS   E. CAUCASUS
BAZ. 3,132,12   BAZ. 3,136
BR. TRANSCAUCASIA
1·5 to 4 ins. long.
Z·E·1905·136

Q5
LM II ARGOS   B·A·K· 261 = OCP 126

P12
-3500 UR

P15
-3500   UR

P2
PRE. EGYPT CDA 33

P3
S·D· 60?   U.C.
EGYPT

P5
INDIA
RECENT

P9
LM II, MYKENAE   GR. III
JHS. 1925, 59

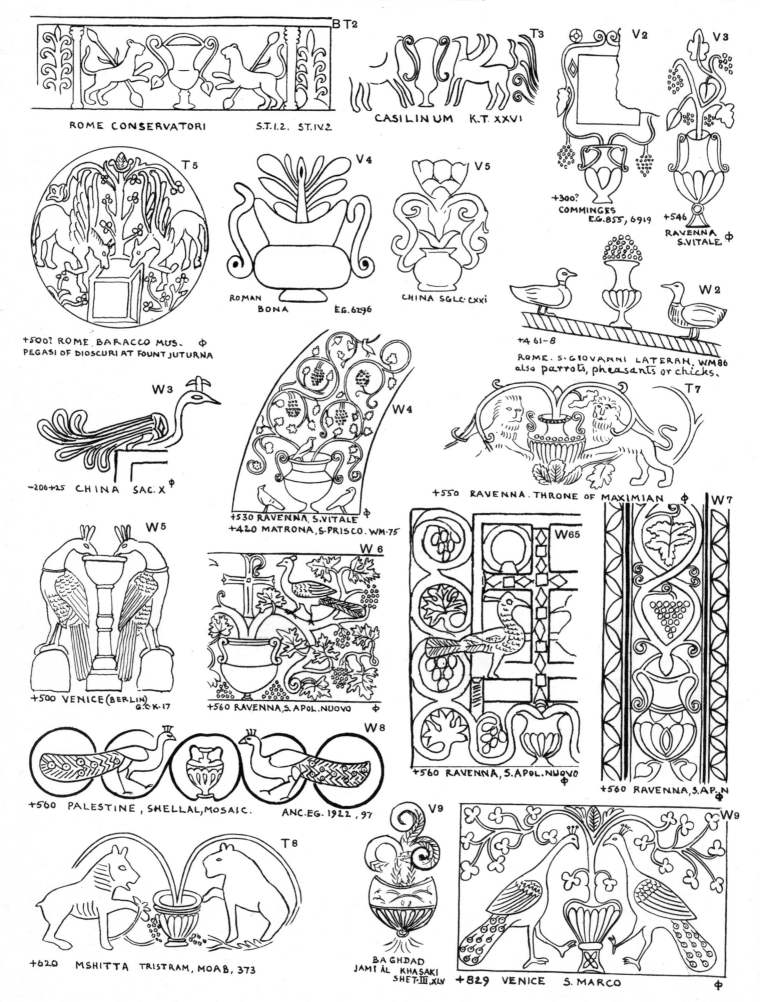

BT2

ROME CONSERVATORI   S.T.I.2. ST.IV.2

CASILINUM   K.T. XXVI

V2

V3

+300? COMMINGES E.G.855, 6919

+546 RAVENNA S.VITALE. Φ

T5

V4

ROMAN BONA   E.G.6296

V5

CHINA SGLC·CXXi

+500? ROME, BARACCO MUS. Φ
PEGASI OF DIOSCURI AT FOUNT JUTURNA

W2

+4 61-8

ROME. S·GIOVANNI LATERAN. WM86
also parrots, pheasants or chicks.

W3

-206+25   CHINA SAC. X Φ

W4

+530 RAVENNA, S.VITALE
+420 MATRONA, S.PRISCO. WM·75

T7

+550 RAVENNA. THRONE OF MAXIMIAN Φ

W7

W5

+500 VENICE (BERLIN)
G.C.K.17

W6

+560 RAVENNA, S.APOL.NUOVO Φ

W65

+560 RAVENNA, S.APOL.NUOVO Φ

+560 RAVENNA, S.AP.N

W8

+560 PALESTINE, SHELLAL, MOSAIC.   ANC.EG. 1922, 97

T8

+620   MSHITTA TRISTRAM, MOAB, 373

V9

BAGHDAD
JAMI AL KHASAKI
SHET.III,XLV

W9

+829 VENICE   S.MARCO Φ

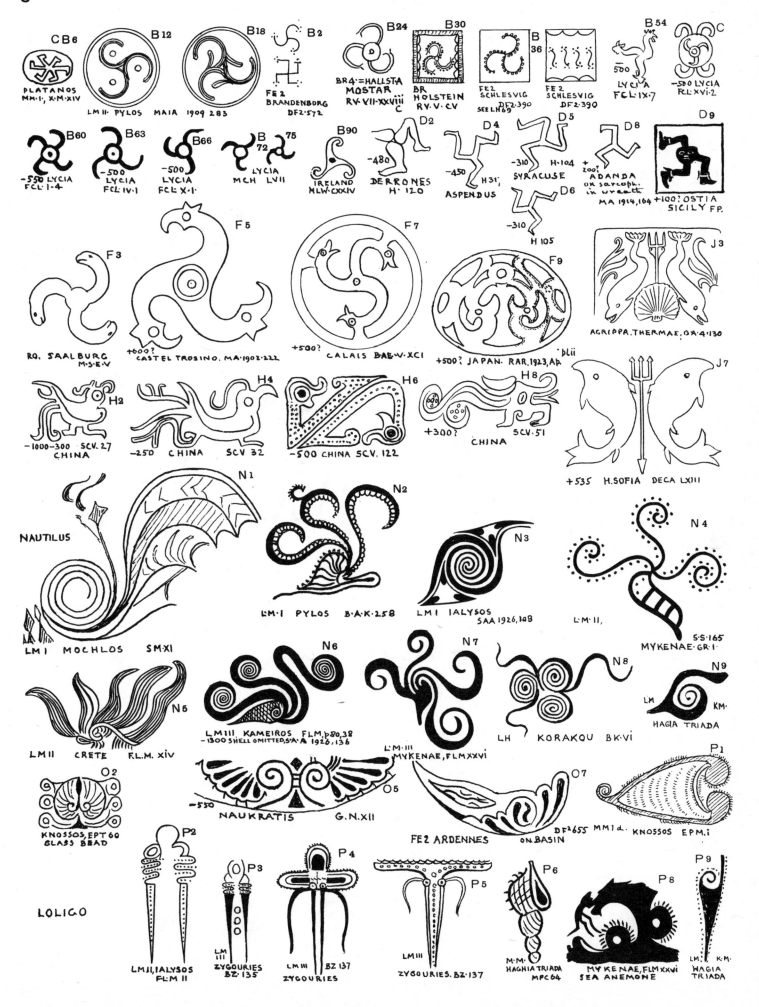

CB6
PLATANOS
MM.I. X.M.XIV

B 12
LM II. PYLOS

MAIA 1909 283

B18

B 2
FE 2
BRANDENBURG
DF2·572

B24
BR4·=HALLSTA
MOSTAR
RV·VII·XXVIII
C

B30
BR
HOLSTEIN
RV.V·CV

B
36
FE2
SCHLESVIG
SEE LH 69 DF2·390

75
FE 2
SCHLESVIG
DF2·390

B 54
-500
LYCIA
FCL·IX·7

C
-500 LYCIA
FCL·XVI·2

B60
-550 LYCIA
FCL I·4

B63
-500
LYCIA
FCL IV·1

B66
-500
LYCIA
FCL X·1·

B
72
LYCIA
MCH LVII

B90
IRELAND
MLW·CXXIV

D2
-480
DERRONES
H·120

D 4
-450
ASPENDUS H·31·

D 5
-310
SYRACUSE H·104

D6
-310
H 105

D8
+200?
ADANDA
ON SARCOPH.
IN UREECT
MA 1914,164

D 9
+100? OSTIA
SICILY FP.

F 3
RO. SAALBURG
M·S·E·V

F 5
+600?
CASTEL TROSINO. MA·1902·222

F 7
+500?
CALAIS BAE·V·XCI

F9
+500? JAPAN. RAR.1923,Ap·blii

J3
AGRIPPA. THERMAE. GA·4·130

H2
-1000-300 SCV. 27
CHINA

H4
-250 CHINA SCV 32

H6
-500 CHINA SCV. 122

H8
+300?
CHINA SCV.51

J7
+535 H.SOFIA DECA LXIII

N1
NAUTILUS
LM I MOCHLOS SM·XI

N2
LM·I PYLOS B·A·K·258

N3
LM I IALYSOS SAA 1926,108

N 4
L·M·II,
MYKENAE· GR·I· S·S·165

N5
LM II CRETE F.L.M. XIV

N6
LM III KAMEIROS FLM·p80,38
-1300 SHELL OMITTED,S·A·A 1926,136

N 7
L·M·III
MYKENAE,FLM XXVI

N8
LH KORAKOU BK·VI

N9
LM   KM·
HAGIA TRIADA

O2
KNOSSOS, EPT 60
GLASS BEAD

O5
-550
NAUKRATIS G.N.XII

O7
FE2 ARDENNES
ON BASIN DF²655

P1
MM I d. KNOSSOS EPM.i

P2
LM II,IALYSOS
FLM II

LOLIGO

P3
LM III
ZYGOURIES
BZ·135

P 4
LM III BZ 137
ZYGOURIES

P5
LM III
ZYGOURIES. BZ·137

P6
M·M·
HAGHIA TRIADA
MPC 64

P 8
MYKENAE,FLM XXVI
SEA ANEMONE

P9
LM· KM·
HAGIA
TRIADA

L·M·IB GOURNIA, BHG.

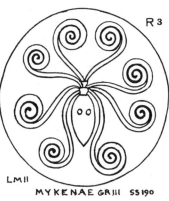

LM II MYKENAE GR III SS 190

LM II MYKENAE, GR III SS·188

KUPHONISIA MGP 307 AMORGOS R6

MM·KAMARES ODE XI R4

DIPYLON MAIA. 1907 XXV R8

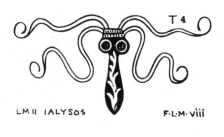

MYKENAE STONE BOX EPH·1888 R26

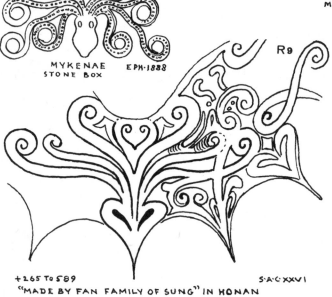

+265 TO 589 S·A·C XXVI "MADE BY FAN FAMILY OF SUNG" IN HONAN

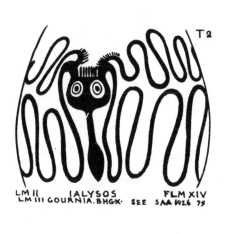

LM II / LM III GOURNIA·BHG X IALYSOS SEE S·A·A 1926 79 FLM XIV T2

·M III MPC·127 S2

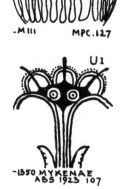

~1350 MYKENAE ABS 1923 107 U1

LM II IALYSOS F·L·M·viii T4

LM II IALYSOS FLM·ii T5

LOS MILLARES SPAIN S·O·O·iii T6

LM II IALYSOS FLM ii U2 / LM·HAGIA TRIADA K·M· U3

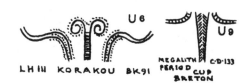

LH III KORAKOU BK91 U6 / MEGALITH PERIOD CUP BRETON C·D·133 U9

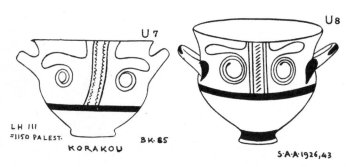

LH III =1150 PALEST. KORAKOU BK·85 U7 / S·A·A 1926,43 U8

CRETE M·S·X X2 / HITTITE H.H.135 X3

ORSOVA M·B·H·1912,15,16 X5 X6 / KNOSSOS INLAY E·P·T·40 X8

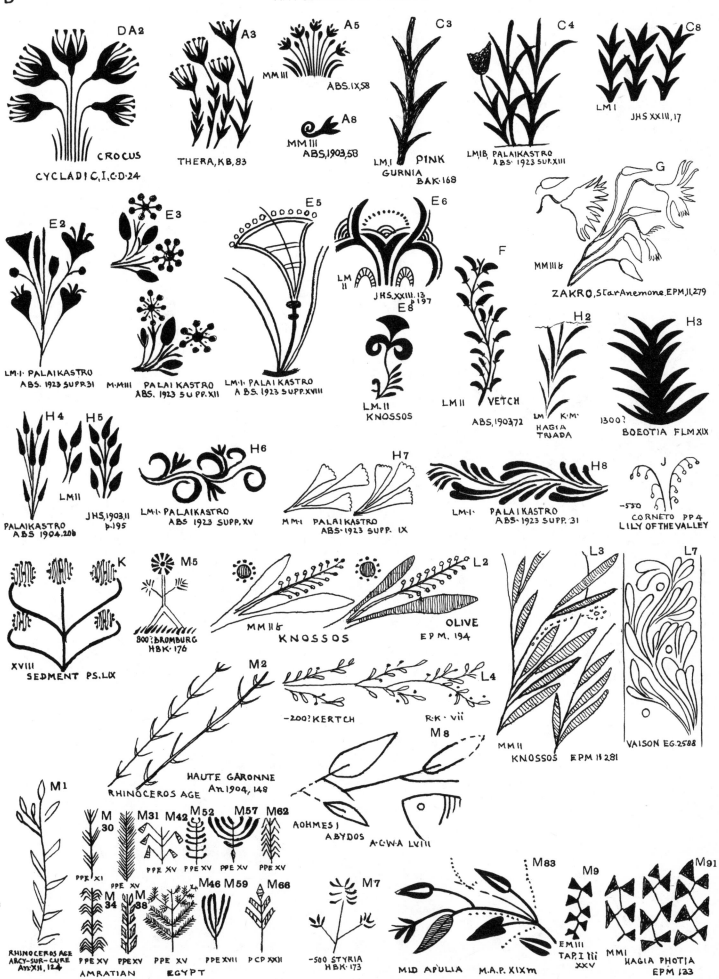

DA2
CROCUS
CYCLADIC, I, C·D·24

A3
THERA, KB, 83

A5
MM III
ABS.IX,58

A8
MM III
ABS,1903,58

C3
PINK
GURNIA
BAK·168
LM.I

C4
LMIB, PALAIKASTRO
ABS· 1923 SUP.XIII

C8
LM I
JHS XXIII, 17

E2
LM·I· PALAIKASTRO
ABS. 1923 SUPR.31

E3
M·MIII PALAIKASTRO
ABS. 1923 SUPP. XII

E5
LM·I· PALAIKASTRO
A BS· 1923 SUPP.XVIII

E6
LM
II
JHS.XXIII.13
p·197

E8
LM·II
KNOSSOS

F
VETCH
LM II
ABS, 1903.72

G
MMIIIb
ZAKRO, Star Anemone. EPM,II,279

H2
LM K·M·
HAGIA
TRIADA

H3
1300?
BOEOTIA FLM XIX

H4
PALAIKASTRO
ABS 1904.20b

H5
LMII
JHS,1903,11
p·195

H6
LM·I· PALAIKASTRO
ABS 1923 SUPP, XV

H7
MMI PALAIKASTRO
ABS·1923 SUPP. IX

H8
LM·I· PALAIKASTRO
ABS·1923 SUPP. 31

J
-550
CORNETO PP4
LILY OF THE VALLEY

K
XVIII
SEDMENT PS.LIX

M5
800? BROMBURG
HBK·176

L2
MM IIb
KNOSSOS
OLIVE
EPM. 194

L3

L7

M2
HAUTE GARONNE
An 1904, 148
RHINOCEROS AGE

L4
-200? KERTCH
R·K· vii

M8
AOHMES I
ABYDOS
A·C·W·A LVIII

MM II
KNOSSOS EPM II 281

VAISON EG.2588

M1
RHINOCEROS AGE
ARCY-SUR-CURE
An XII, 124

M
30
PPE XI

M31
PPE XV

M42
PPE XV

M52
PPE XV

M57
PPE XV

M62
PPE XV

M
34
PPE XV
AMRATIAN

M
38
PPE XV

M46
PPE XV
EGYPT

M59
PPE XVII

M66
P CP XXII

M7
-500 STYRIA
HBK·173

M83
MID APULIA
M.A.P. XIXm

M9
EM III
TAP.I IIi
XXV

M91
MMI
HAGIA PHOTIA
EPM 133

D

DN

O2

O3
+50? MAINZ   LA.V. 502

O4
NEUMAGEN E.G 5220

O5
+600?
SASSANIDE BOWL. SP.CXXIII

O7
+488 DIPTYCH
SI VIDIUS
DCD VIII

O9
L·M·   K·M·
HAGIA TRIADA

LM II
PYLOS MAIA 1909 XXII

-100
COMMAGENE
ON DRESS
S P. LVII

LOTUS

P
1450   (BERLIN)   M.S.9

Q2
XVIII AMARNA
P.A.XIX

Q4
XVIII   GUROB P·I·K·XX

Q7

Q9
+589 TO 616   CHINA   SAC XLVII

-1180 GERAR   P.G.I

R1
ARCHAIC.SUSA.DCLXV,8

R4
KOUYUNJIK

R6
-730 NIMRUD EMBROIDERY, LN.XLIV

R7
ASHUR   ACA,XIV

R9
LITOY KURGAN LOW DNIEPER
SKYTHO-SARM· RV·XIII,XXXIV A

S2
-600
CORTONA   MA 1925,110

S4
CAPUA   KT·41

S5
CAPUA   KT42

S6
TORCELLO   Φ

T
-700 RHODES   KB.115

S8
CAPUA   KT.XXXIV

U
-600 SPARTA,ABS.1909.31

W
+500 RAVENNA
THEODORIC. MA 1916
755

Y4
-600 CORNETO, PP.2

Y5
-550 NAUKRATIS PNKVIII

Y7
-550 NAUKRATIS   PNK. VIII
S.APULIA

Z2
XVIII AMARNA   P.A. X

Z8
450 BOLOGNA   R·I·35
MA XXVIII

X
-600 NAUKRATIS   PNK.VI,&XIII

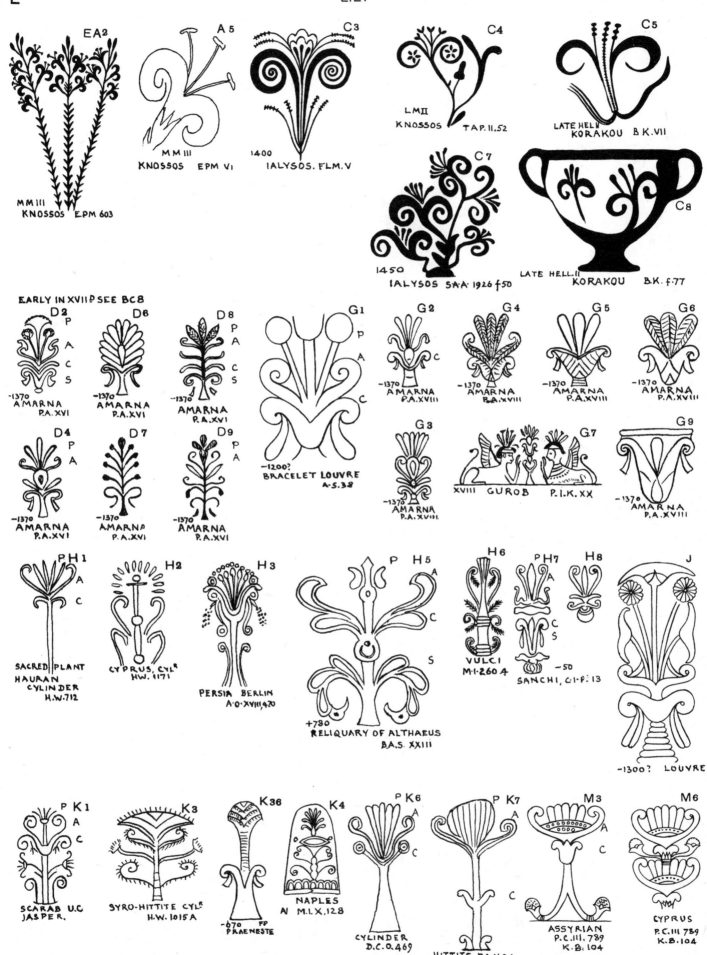

EA2

MM III
KNOSSOS   E.P.M 603

A 5

MM III
KNOSSOS   EPM VI

C 3

1400
IALYSOS. FLM. V

C 4

LM II
KNOSSOS   TAP. II.52

C 5

LATE HELL
KORAKOU   B K.VII

C 7

1450
IALYSOS   SAA 1926 f50

C 8

LATE HELL.II
KORAKOU   B.K. f.77

EARLY IN XVIII? SEE BC8

D 2
P
A
C
S

−1370
AMARNA
P.A. XVI

D 6

−1370
AMARNA
P.A. XVI

D 8
P
A
C
S

−1370
AMARNA
P.A. XVI

D 4
P
A

−1370
AMARNA
P.A. XVI

D 7

−1370
AMARNA
P.A. XVI

D 9
P
A

−1370
AMARNA
P.A. XVI

G 1
P
A
C

−1200?
BRACELET LOUVRE
A.S. 38

G 2
C

−1370
AMARNA
P.A. XVIII

G 3

−1370
AMARNA
P.A. XVIII

G 4

−1370
AMARNA
B.A. XVIII

G 5

−1370
AMARNA
P.A. XVIII

G 6

−1370
AMARNA
P.A. XVIII

G 7

XVIII   GUROB   P.I.K. XX

G 9

−1370
AMARNA
P.A. XVIII

PH 1
A
C

SACRED PLANT
HAURAN
CYLINDER
H.W. 712

H 2

CYPRUS. CYL?
H.W. 1171

H 3

PERSIA BERLIN
A.O. XVIII, 470

P H 5
A
C
S

+780
RELIQUARY OF ALTHAEUS
B.A.S. XXIII

H 6

VULCI
M.I. 260 4

P H 7
C
S

−50
SANCHI. C.I.P. 13

H 8

J

−1300?   LOUVRE

P K 1
A
C

SCARAB U.C
JASPER.

K 3

SYRO-HITTITE CYL?
H.W. 1015 A

K 36

−670   FP
PRAENESTE

K 4

NAPLES
N M.L X. 128

P K 6
A
C

CYLINDER
D.C.O. 469

P K 7
A
C

HITTITE. P.A.H. 26

M 3
A
C

ASSYRIAN
P.C. III, 789
K.B. 104

M 6

CYPRUS
P.C. III 789
K.B. 104

M7
CYPRUS. LOUVRE
K.B.108 D.C.P.232

N
KOUYUNJIK

P1
? +200
UNIT OF NECKLACE
KYRENIA, CYPRUS
S.A. VIII

P3
CRETE. MS. XI

P5
TAMASSOS. MAK.323

P7
CRETE MS.XI

P A P9
CYPRUS   M.A.K. 322

Q2
SUPERPOSED IN
PILE. RUAD
+WINGED SPHINX
ASSYRIAN STYLE
R.M.P. IV

Q4
-700?
MARINO LAZIALE
TOMB 16 BRONZE
1923   K.M.

Q5
FALERII   M.1.311.11.   K.M.

Q6
-600?
CAPENA (ROMA) K.M.

Q8
-600?
MUS. GREG.

Q9
F.P. - -700? ATHENS. K.B.116

S2
+100? MATHURA. BOSTON. Φ

S3
VULCI   M.1.264.8

S4 S5
-670
BARBERINI TOMB, PRAENESTE
IMPRESSED GOLD
M.A.A. V 8

S6
MARZABOTTO. M.1.107,15

S7
-600?
CAPENA (ROMA) K.M.

S8
-600?
CAPENA   K.M.

S9
DAN II RÖSSEN
-2000 CDP 118

T2
B.MUS.
TARQINII
MKE 89

T3
CORNETO   M.1.294

T4
+400 NICHOMACHORUM
DIPTYCH DC.D. LIV

T5
CAPUA. K.T.109

T6
-300? MARNE   H.J. II.184

T66
-650?
M.1.243

T7
CAPUA
K.T.XXV

T74
-600?
CRETE   K.B.115

T8
M.1.1914
VETULONIA, LICTOR.

T85
GHIUSI. PANIA   M.1.225.7

T9
+90
CRYPTOPORTICUS
PALATINE
M.A.A, IV, XI

T93
+50
SEBASTIANO CATACOMB, ROME.

T95
F.P. +130
COL. TRAIAN, G.A. 117

T97
+150
PANCRATII TOMB
M.A.A. IV. XXXIII

Y1
+620. ANAHITA
TAQ I BUSTAN
DRESS HFD. LXV

Y2
+546
S. VITALE, RAVEN
R.S. 79

Y3
+546 S. VITALE Φ
RAVENNA

Y4
+450 AJANTA, C.I.P.31
INDIA

Y5
+525 DIPTYCH
PHILOXENUS
DC D XXX

Y9
DENMARK. M.A.K.224

Y6
+706
S. MARIA, ANTICA. ROME   Φ

Y7
S. MARIA ANTICA
ROME
F.P.

Y8
+770
S. MARIA CIVIDALE   Φ

FA1

X DYN   QAU   PQi

A3

-730 NIMRUD EMBROIDERY   L.N. VI

A4

NIMRUD   BRIT. MUS. P.0.9

A9

LITOY KURGAN LON DNIEPR
SCYTHO-SARM· RVXIII 344A

A5

ASSYRIA BM

A6

SIBERIA
MPO III 224

A7

THRONE ROOM BABYLON
KWE 64

A8

-500?
SUSA LION FRIEZE   S.P. XXXIX

B1

-570 AOHMES
MON. LEYDEN
II, LXVII

B2

KOLDEWY BABYLON, 130
KWE 64

B3

-700,600   MEGIDDO

B4

CHIUSI. (FLOR.)   DA.83

B5

-600? CORNETO   Φ

B8

MONTE CALVARIO
NS. 1905. 233

B9

-670 CAERE
R·M·E

C2

M.I. 244

C7

-700
CU MA. MA, 1913 XLVIII

C12

NIMRUD, MAK. 963

C17

-600?
CERVETRI   SEDIA CORSINI
MA 1916, 458, V

C22

FALERII   M.I. 327. 13

C27

CHIUSI. PANIA   M·I·225.7.

C32

-670 CAERE   RME

C37

PRAENESTE, BARBERINI TOMB
ROUGH IVORY.   M·A·A·V.10

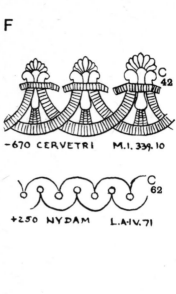

-670 CERVETRI   M.I. 339. 10   C42

FALERII. M.I. 319.2   C47

FALERII   M.I. 311,18   C52

FALERII   M.I. 311,19   C57

+250 NYDAM   L.A·IV. 71   C62

HANGEBEKENS. SWEDEN   M.L.S. V   C67

CAPUA   KT. XXVIII   C72

NAGY SZENT MIKLOS   GOLD BOTTLE   S.A. 65   C77

+800 AGAUNE, RELIQUARY (SEE DACIAN QC 4,5)   BAS. XXV   C82

MONTE CALVARIO   N.S. 1905, 232 fig. 26   C87

ACANTHUS

AKANTHOS BRACT NATURAL J·I· 1896, 149   D1

-400? ATHENS. J·I·1896 AKROPOLIS 151   D2

-400 ERECHTHEION. KB.138   D3

-500 CAULONIA, MA, 1923, IV   D4

-400? CAULONIA. MA.1923,VII   D5

CAPUA.   KT. XXX   D6

CAPUA   KT.XXV   D7

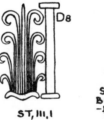

ST, III, 1   D8

SITULA BOLDU-DOLFIN B.C. 66   D9

CORNETO   WEM. VIII   E2

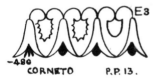

CORNETO   P.P. 13.   E3

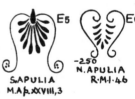

SAPULIA M.A.t.XXVIII,3   E5

-250 N.APULIA R.M.I.46   E6

CAPUA   KT. 45   E7

+160 BAALBEK, ALTAR COURT.   F2

YUDINA M.M. XV   F3

S.B.I,103   +200 COTTAEUM J RS 1925 XXIII   F4

+640 SYRACUSE JAMB   F6

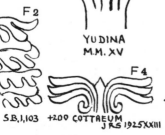

+640 SYRACUSE JAMB   F7

+1050 S. CLEMENTE, ROME. ALEXIS   F8

FOSCHERARI BOLOGNA   F9

FLEUR-DE-LIS

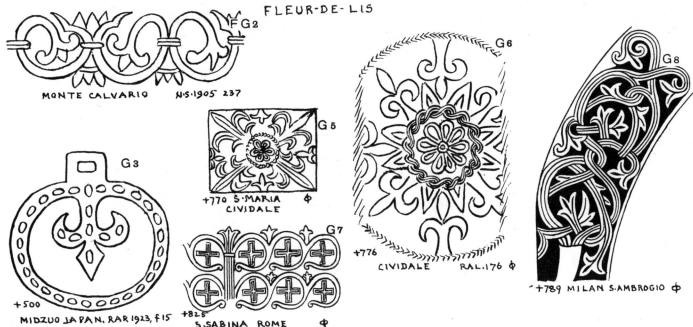

FG2

MONTE CALVARIO   N·S·1905 237

G3

+500
MIDZUO JAPAN, RAR 1923, f15

G5
+770 S·MARIA
CIVIDALE   Φ

G7
+825
S·SABINA ROME   Φ

G6
+776
CIVIDALE   RAL·176 Φ

G8
+789 MILAN S·AMBROGIO Φ

FORMAL FLOWERS

H1
LM II
KNOSSOS EPM II 285

H2
SEE LS5b
LM II
KNOSSOS, A, 1914 66

H3
LATE
HEL. II
KORAKOU, BK· VII

H4
MYKENAE, JHS, XXIV

H5
CRETE
MOSSO KB. 84

H6
MM II PALAIKASTRO
ABS. 1923 SUPP. 26

H7
LM·III·PALAIKASTRO

H8
ABS. 1923 SUPP. XXIII

H9
−1200
SPATA   FLM·XVII

J3
−670
CUMA   R·M·I· 53

J6
−400 ARCHENA, MURCIA R·V·I xlii

J4
−670
CUMA   M·A·1913,30; R·M·I·pl·36

J5

J7
MM III KNOSSOS FAIENCE
ABS 1903 67

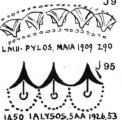

J8
LM II
BSA1903
p311, 9.

J9
LM III PYLOS, MAIA 1909 290

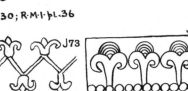

J73
XVII KAMES SPEAR
ESB 30

J74
MYKENAE

J95
1450 IALYSOS, SAA 1926, 53

FK1
MM·I· PALAIKASTRO
A.B.S. 1923 SUPP. VI.

K2
MM PHAESTOS
MPC, 13

K3
XVIII AMARNA
P.A. XXVII

K35
LMIIIa IALYSOS FLM VIII

K4
XVIII L·M·II AMARNA P·A·XVIII

K5
XVIII AMARNA
PA. XXVII

K6
LM1a KNOSSOS EPM II 285 -1400

K63
IALYSOS, FLM, III

K68
MYKENAE FLM, XXXV

K7
-1150?
CRETE MA. 1889, 230, II

K8
MYKENAE FLM, XXXIV

K9
-1400
IALYSOS, FLM, VI

L1
XII EGYPT UC

L2
CRETE, EPM 15

L3
XII SCARAB EPM, 150

L4
MM I. CRETE M.S. XII

L5
1400 IALYSOS, FLM III AND IX

L6

L7
1350 ALIKI, ATTICA FLM, XVIII

L8
LM III COZZO, SYRACUSE

MA, 1893 I, DCP 153

L9
CROSS OF JUSTIN + SOPHIA LATERAN DECA IXI

M1
MM I. PLATANOS X·M·XIV

M2
MM I. PALAIKASTRO ABS·1923 SUPP. VIII

M25
-1400? CRETE
FLM XIV

M31
ARCEVIA MA. 1900, 694

M35

M36

M38
LM II KNOSSOS HOUSES TAP. II 60

M50

M60
LM.I.
MA. 1902. VIII

M65
+620 TAQI BUSTAN S.P. XCII

M70
FRANK WIESBADEN AFW 160

M75
+660 FRIESLAND, A.A.S. 295

M90
+800 SWISS BINDING B.A.S. XXVx

M50
POMPEI B.P.

M54
AQUILEIA RS. 83

M58
+630 CROWN OF SWINTILA. RS. 100

N2
+810 RAVENNA S. APOL. CLASSE Φ

N3
BAALBEK, ALTAR COURT SB. 1·83

N4
+300? GRADINA MBH. 1906, 244

N5
+560 RAVENNA, S. APOLLINARE NUOVO Φ

N7
+500 RAVENNA ARIAN BAPTISTY Φ

N9

850 DEIR ES SURJANI EGYPT GCK. 60

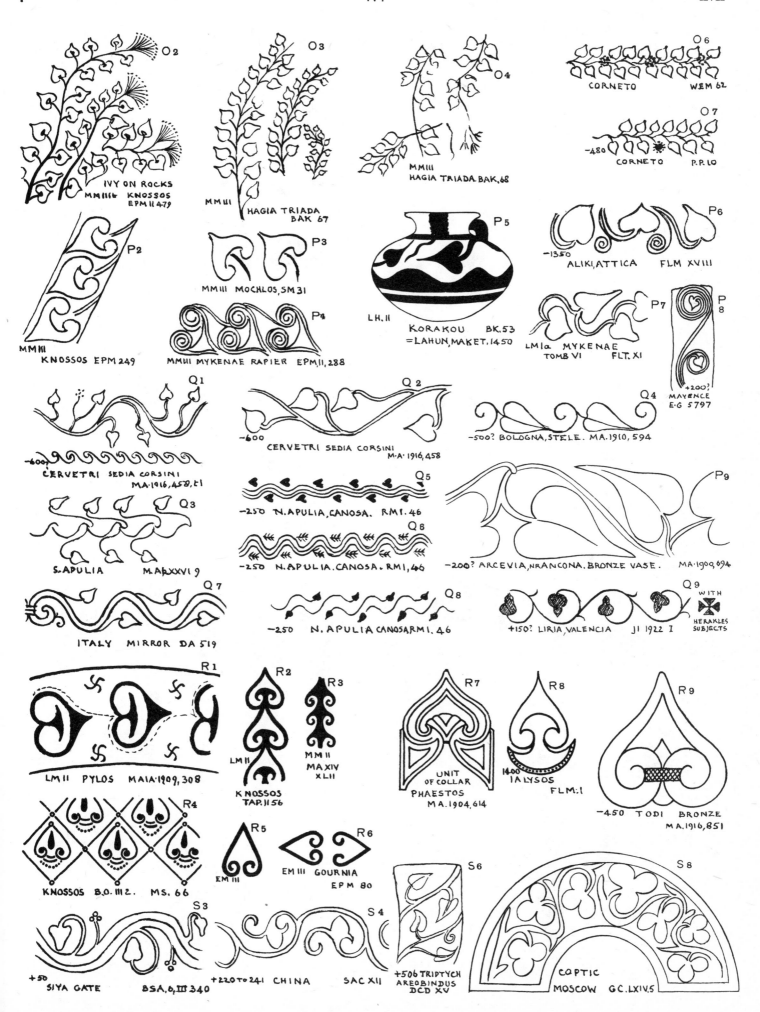

O2

O3

O4

O6
CORNETO   WEM 62

O7
-480   CORNETO   P.P.LO

IVY ON ROCKS
MMIIIb KNOSSOS
EPM II 479

MMIII

HAGIA TRIADA
BAK 67

MMIII
HAGIA TRIADA BAK.68

P2

P3
MMIII MOCHLOS, SM 31

P5
LH.II
KORAKOU   BK.53
= LAHUN, MAKET. 1450

P6
-1350
ALIKI, ATTICA   FLM XVIII

P7
LMIa MYKENAE
TOMB VI   FLT. XI

P8
+200?
MAYENCE
E.G 5797

MMII
KNOSSOS EPM 249

P4
MMIII MYKENAE RAPIER   EPM II, 288

Q1
-600
CERVETRI SEDIA CORSINI
MA.1916,458,t.1

Q2
-600
CERVETRI SEDIA CORSINI
M.A. 1916, 458

Q4
-500? BOLOGNA, STELE. MA.1910, 594

Q3
S.APULIA   M.A.XXVI 9

Q5
-250 N.APULIA, CANOSA. RMI. 46

Q6
-250 N.APULIA.CANOSA. RMI, 46

P9
-200? ARCEVIA, NR ANCONA. BRONZE VASE.   MA.1909,694

Q7
ITALY   MIRROR DA 519

Q8
-250   N. APULIA CANOSA RMI. 46

Q9
+150? LIRIA, VALENCIA   JI 1922 I
WITH
HERAKLES
SUBJECTS

R1
LM II PYLOS   MAIA·1909, 308

R2

R3
LM II
MM II
MA XIV
XLII
KNOSSOS
TAP.II 56

R7
UNIT
OF COLLAR
PHAESTOS
MA. 1904, 614

R8
1400
IALYSOS
FLM:1

R9
-450 TODI BRONZE
MA.1916,851

R4
KNOSSOS B.O. III 2.   MS. 66

R5
EM III

R6
EM III GOURNIA
EPM 80

S3
+50
SIYA GATE   BSA.6,III 340

S4
+220 TO 241 CHINA   SAC XII

S6
+506 TRIPTYCH
AREOBINDUS
DCD XV

S8
COPTIC
MOSCOW   GC.LXIV,5

T7 +528 CHINA, PILLAR. SGLC LXXXV

U1 +50 SIYA GATE   BSA.6.III 342

U2 BAWYT   GC

T1

U3 GERANIUM NATURAL   FP

III DYN MEYDUM SENEFRU P.WM XX

U4 +500 OXYRHYNKHOS PTC XLVII

U5 +540 DIPTYCH JUSTINUS DCD XXXIV EARLIEST PERSIAN

U9

U6 +525 CONSULAR DIPTYCH DCD XLII

U7 +525 DIPTYCH PHILOXENUS DCD·XXX

U8 +620 TAQI BUSTAN. SP.XCII ADAPTED FROM SUSA PALMETTO FA8

+620 TAQI BUSTAN, S.P. XC.

PERSIAN FOLIAGE SEE LXXXVI

FOLIAGE CHANGED TO SKIRL, PU6

V1 +650 OR 750 S. MARIA ANTIQUA ROME F.P.

V2 +825 SCHEME OF S. SABINA BELOW SCHEME OF SKIRL FOLIAGE V3

V4

V5 +789 MILAN, S. AMBROGIO Φ

V3 +825 ROME S. SABINA   Φ

+827 ROME S. GIORGIO VEL. F.P.

V6 BACK OF CROSS Φ

V7

V8 +840 CROSS OF LUDOVICUS + LOTHARIUS, BOLOGNA Φ SKIRL BROKEN LOOSE

+800 BUDRIO Φ

CAST IN BOLOGNA. BY BP. VITALIS +789-814

PETALS GROUPED TO SKIRL

V9 BOLOGNA REUSED IN FOSCHERARI TOMB. Φ

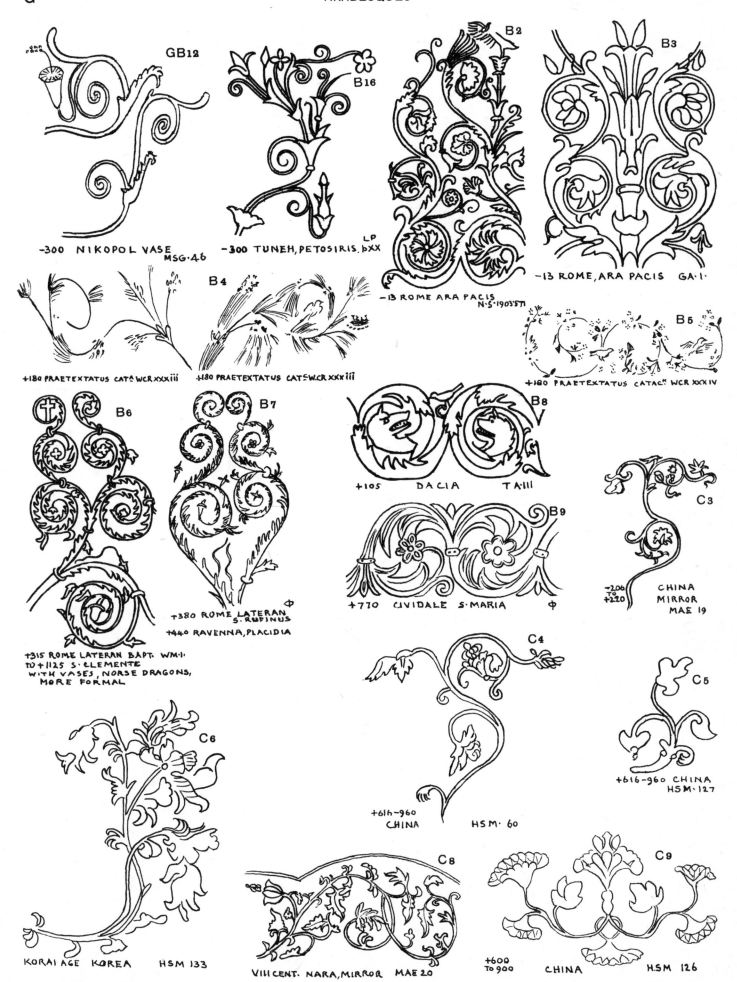

GB12

-300 NIKOPOL VASE
MSG·46

B16

-300 TUNEH, PETOSIRIS. bXX
LP

B2

-13 ROME ARA PACIS
N·S·1903·571

B3

-13 ROME, ARA PACIS   GA·1·

B4

+180 PRAETEXTATUS CAT⁰ WCR xxxiii

+180 PRAETEXTATUS CAT⁰ W.CR xxxiii

B5

+180 PRAETEXTATUS CATAC^N WCR XXXIV

B6

B7

+315 ROME LATERAN BAPT. WM·1·
TO +1125 S·CLEMENTE
WITH VASES, NORSE DRAGONS,
MORE FORMAL

+380 ROME LATERAN
S·RUFINUS
+440 RAVENNA, PLACIDIA

B8

+105   DACIA   TA·III·

B9

+770   CIVIDALE S·MARIA

C3

-206
TO
+220
CHINA
MIRROR
MAE 19

C4

+616-960
CHINA   HSM· 60

C5

+616-960 CHINA
HSM·127

C6

KORAI AGE KOREA   HSM 133

C8

VIII CENT. NARA, MIRROR   MAE 20

C9

+600
TO 900   CHINA   H.S.M 126

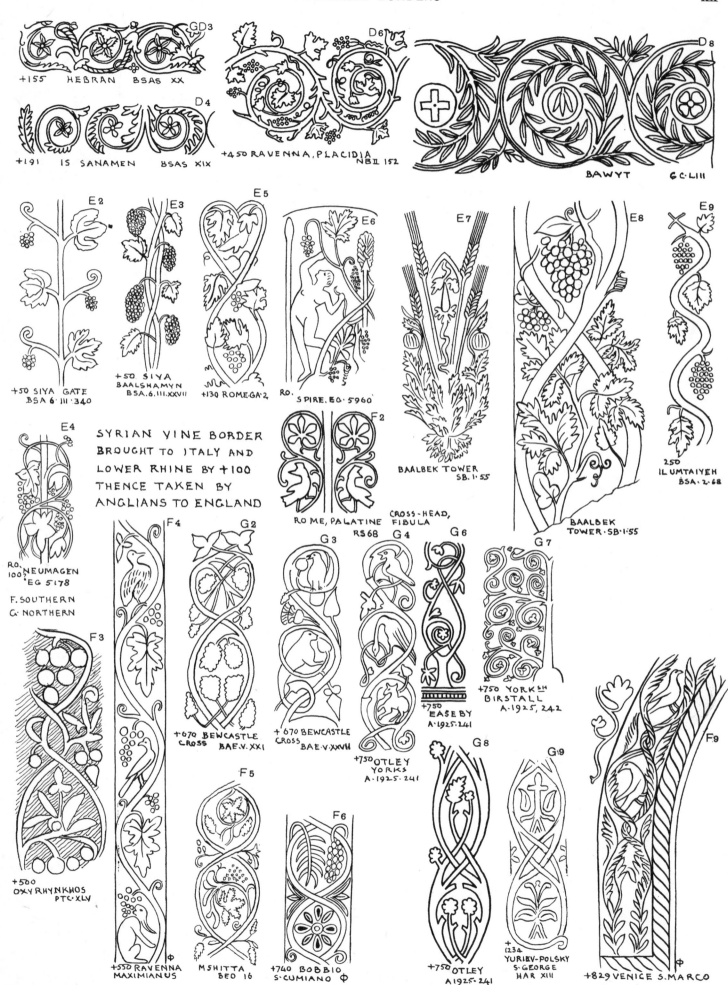

GD3
+155 HEBRAN BSAS XX

D4
+191 IS SANAMEN BSAS XIX

D6
+450 RAVENNA, PLACIDIA NB II 152

D8
BAWYT   GC·LIII

E2
+50 SIYA GATE BSA 6·III·340

E3
+50 SIYA BAALSHAMYN BSA.6.III.XXVII

E5
+130 ROME·GA·2

E6
RO. SPIRE. EG. 5960

E7
BAALBEK TOWER SB.1·55

E8
BAALBEK TOWER·SB·1·55

E9
250 IL UMTAIYEH BSA.2·68

E4
RO. NEUMAGEN 100? EG 5178

SYRIAN VINE BORDER
BROUGHT TO ITALY AND
LOWER RHINE BY +100
THENCE TAKEN BY
ANGLIANS TO ENGLAND

F. SOUTHERN
G. NORTHERN

F2
ROME, PALATINE CROSS-HEAD, FIBULA RS68

F3
+500 OXYRHYNKHOS PTC·XLV

F4
+670 BEWCASTLE CROSS BAE.V.XXI

G2

G3
+670 BEWCASTLE CROSS BAE.V.XXVII

G4
+750 OTLEY YORKS A·1925·241

G6
+750 EASEBY A·1925·241

G7
+750 YORK S? BIRSTALL A·1925, 242

F5

F6
+740 BOBBIO S·CUMIANO Φ

G8
+750 OTLEY A·1925·241

G9
+1234 YURIEV-POLSKY S·GEORGE HAR XIII

F9
+829 VENICE S.MARCO

+550 RAVENNA MAXIMIANUS

M SHITTA BEO 16

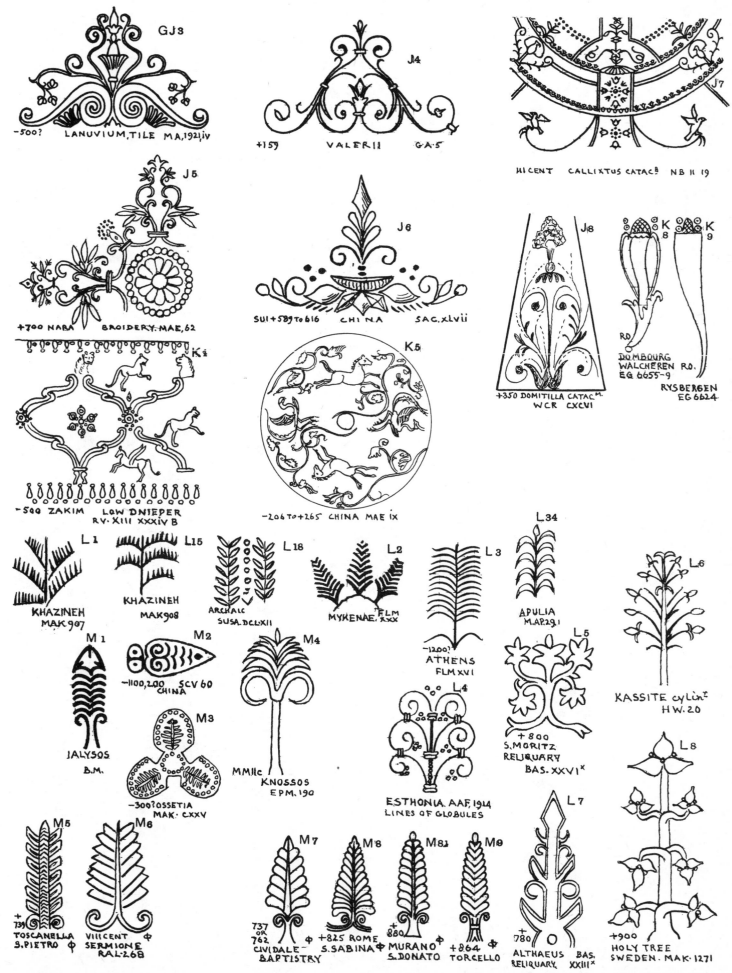

GJ3
−500? LANUVIUM, TILE MA,1921,iv

J4
+159 VALERII GA·5

J7
HI CENT CALLIXTUS CATAC? NB II 19

J5
+700 NARA BROIDERY MAE,62

J6
SUI +589 TO 616 CHINA SAC. XLVII

J18
+350 DOMITILLA CATAC M. WCR CXCVI

K8 K9
R.D. DOMBOURG WALCHEREN R.D. EG 6655-9 RYSBERGEN EG 6624

K2
−500 ZAKIM LOW DNIEPER RV. XIII XXXIV B

K5
−206 TO +265 CHINA MAE ix

L1 KHAZINEH MAK 907
L15 KHAZINEH MAK 908
L18 ARCHAIC SUSA DCLXII
L2 MYKENAE. FLM XXX
L3 −1200? ATHENS FLM XVI
L34 APULIA M. AP.29.1
L6

L5 +800 S.MORITZ RELIQUARY BAS. XXVI x

KASSITE cylinr HW.20

L8

M1 JALYSOS B.M.
M2 −1100,200 SCV 60 CHINA
M3 −300? OSSETIA MAK. CXXV
M4 MMIIc KNOSSOS EPM.190
L4 ESTHONIA. AAF,1914 LINES OF GLOBULES
L7 +780 ALTHAEUS BAS. RELIQUARY XXIII x

M5
M6
+739 TOSCANELLA S.PIETRO φ
VIIICENT SERMIONE RAL.268 φ

M7 737 OR 762 CIVIDALE BAPTISTRY φ
M8 +825 ROME S. SABINA φ
M81 +880 MURANO S. DONATO φ
M9 +864 TORCELLO φ

+900 HOLY TREE SWEDEN. MAK.1271

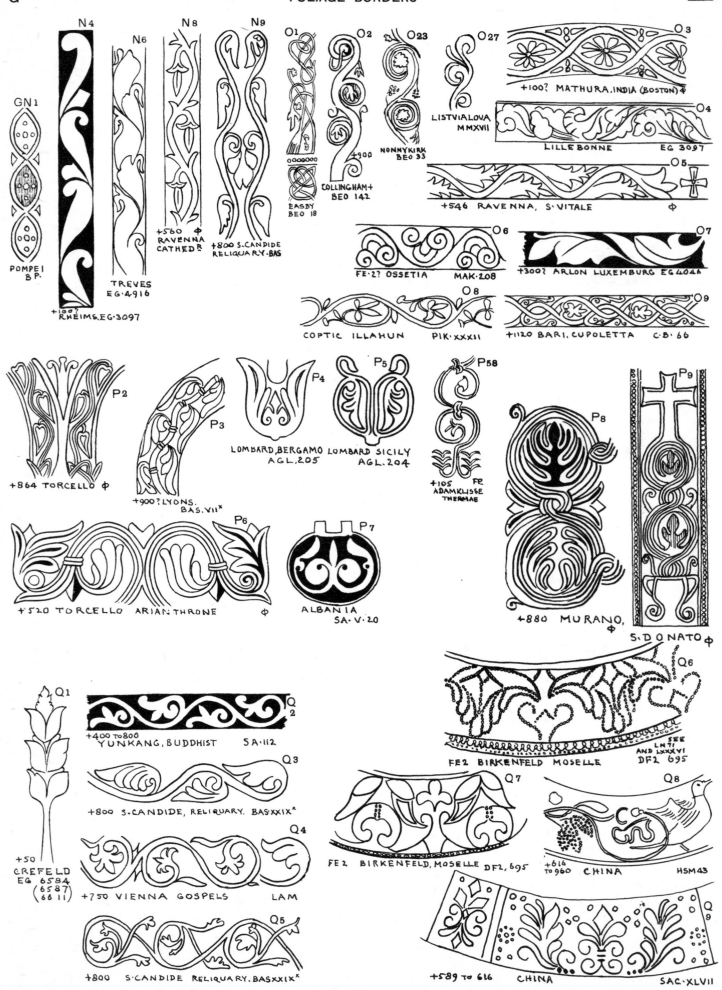

N4

N6

N8

N9

O1

O2

O23

O27

O3
+100? MATHURA, INDIA (BOSTON) Φ

GN1

LISTVIALOVA
MMXVII

NONNYKIRK
BEO 33

O4
LILLEBONNE   EG 3097

+900

COLLINGHAM+
BEO 142

O5
+546 RAVENNA, S. VITALE   Φ

EASBY
BEO 18

POMPEI
B P.

+560 Φ
RAVENNA
CATHEDR

+800 S. CANDIDE
RELIQUARY. BAS

TREVES
EG. 4916

+100?
RHEIMS. EG. 3097

O6
FE.2? OSSETIA   MAK. 208

O7
+300? ARLON LUXEMBURG EG 4046

O8
COPTIC ILLAHUN   PIK. XXXII

O9
+1120 BARI, CUPOLETTA   C.B. 66

P2
+864 TORCELLO Φ

P3
+900? LYONS.
BAS. VII x

P4
LOMBARD, BERGAMO
AGL. 205

P5
LOMBARD SICILY
AGL. 204

P58
+105 FR
ADAMKLISSE
THERMAE

P8

P9

P6
+520 TORCELLO ARIAN THRONE   Φ

P7
ALBANIA
SA. V. 20

+880 MURANO,
Φ

S. DONATO Φ

Q1

Q2
+400 TO 800
YUNKANG, BUDDHIST   SA. 112

Q6
FE2 BIRKENFELD MOSELLE   SEE
LN 71
AND LXXXVI
DF2 695

Q3
+800 S. CANDIDE, RELIQUARY. BAS XXIX x

Q7

Q4
+750 VIENNA GOSPELS   LAM

Q8

+50
CREFELD
EG 6584
(6587)
(6611)

FE2 BIRKENFELD, MOSELLE DF2, 695

+616
TO 960 CHINA   HSM43

Q5
+800 S. CANDIDE RELIQUARY. BAS XXIX x

Q9
+589 TO 616   CHINA   SAC. XLVII

S2   MM HI MYKENAE   GRJV   SS 238

S4   -700? IALYSOS PITHOI SAA 1926 222

S5   -700? IALYSOS SAA· 1926 209

S6   LMII ZYGOURIES BZ·129

S7   -1200 TRIPOLYE A. MSG 30 KIEV

S8   LMII·ISOPATA. TDA 64

S9   LMII. ISOPATA. TDA 64

T2   S. APULIA   MA XXVIII·1

T3   LM-I   JHS 1903·3

T6   FALERII   M I. 321. 10

T7   CAPPADOCIA   GCC·1658,31 B

T8   MYKENAE FLM.XXVII

U1   +60 VITALIS, POMPEII JRS.1914.V

U2   +470 CONSULAR DIPTYCH DCD XXXVIII

U14   +60 POMPEII   JRS.1914,VIII

U3   +800 S.MORITZ. RELIQUARY BAS XXV ×

U4   -250 CANOSA, N. APULIA   RMI. pl.46

U45   S. APULIA   M. AB·XXVIII·6

U5   -250 CANOSA N.APULIA   RMI. pl.46

U8   -300 SCYTHIAN. FRONT. R. I. G

U6   +200 COTTAEUM JRS.1925,XXIII

U66   +50 SIYA   BSA. 6. 340

U7   +580 ALFRISTON A.A·S·300

U9   CHINA   MAE.49

V1   ARCHAIC TELL LO DCL·1·9

V3   -3500 UR

V2   -1150? CRETE MA·1889,230,ii

V3   VULCI   M·I. 260.6

V4   PALAEKASTRO LM MA·1904,571 LMIII·AJA·1941·VI ERGANOS, CRETE

V5   MYKENAE Φ GRAVE IV

V56   BEFORE -3500 UR

V6   +100? MATHURA, INDIA (BOSTON) Φ

V7   +250 VASE, EGYPT. P.E.XXXIII

V9   +440 RAVENNA   GALLA PLACIDIA Φ

V8   TENE HELMET, BERRU   M·F· S SEE ES6

GW1

+616 TO 960   CHINA   HSM 58

+450

W5

HASLINGFIELD, CAMBS. A·A·S·17

W2

W4

-206 to +25   CHINA   SAC·XX

+220 TO 41   CHINA   SAC XIII

W6

+220 TO 241   CHINA   SACXI

W7

+600 (SUI or TANG)   CHINA   SEE LRB   HS M.108

W8

+265 TO 300   CHINA   SAC XLII

W9

+589 TO 616   CHINA   SAC XLV

X2

GOTHIC
RECESVINTH
CLUNY. OTP.II,11

X5

TARQUINII
MKE 204

X7

MMIIa KNOSSOS
KAMARES WARE
EPM iii

X9

+700?
QASR HARANEH   JSA III 15

Z1

LM·I· PALAIKASTRO
ABS. 1905,276

Z2

BR.
KOBAN
MAK·XXIV

Z8

+546 RAVENNA
S. VITALE   Φ

X3

BRONZE AXE
KOBAN
MAK 25

X6

PETROASSA
COLLAR OTP.II·74

X8

+500 HONAN
SSC XCIII

Y2

-700?

CUMA
MA,1913,XLII

Y3

POMPEII   B.P.

Y5

FE.1
GRANDATE
COMO B.C.56

Y6

HALLSTATT
B.C.54

Z3

MM II KNOSSOS EPM,186

Z4

+825
ROME, S.SABINA   Φ

Z5

+200?
BAIA   MA.1922,138

Z6

MM II KNOSSOS, EPM 186

Z7

MM I, KNOSSOS
EPM,186

Z9

+752
CIVIDALE
CROSS OF
PELTRUDIS.

Y8

+1050 S.CLEMENTE, ROME. BENO,   Φ

HA1

BABYLONIA
J.C.B.LIII

A8

-570
NAUKR?
JHS 1924·XI

4

B3

TELL LO, DCL.I,14

B4

ARCHAIC
TELL LO   DCL.I,10

B6

ARCHAIC, SUSA, DCL.XVIII-17

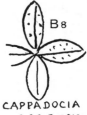

B8

CAPPADOCIA
G CC I 9810

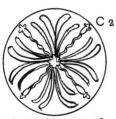

C2

+60 POTTER·MEMOR,
POMPEII. JRS,1914, XIV

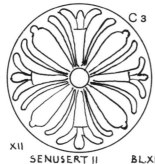

C3

XII
SENUSERT II   BL.XI
XII STEERING OAR, EPM 427B

C6

XVIII AMENEMHAT, THEBES   JOE.41

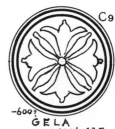

C9

-600?
GELA
MA·1906, 635

D2

MYKENAE
FLM XXVIII

D4

-600
NAUKRATIS
P.NK·IV

D5

-350 PIKERMI ATTICA
RELIEF MAIA,1924,12

D6

WOODCHESTER
L·W· VII

D7

+100?
WORMS
L.A.V,1200a

D8

TAQ I BUSTAN   HFD XV

D9

MIKHAILOF POLAND?
JOAI·1906·32

5

E3

XVIII AMARNA
P.A.XVIII

E4

LM III
ABS.1903, 318,17

E6

-730
NIMRUD
BELT,
L.N.XXVI

E8

-700?
MELOS
K B,113

6

F4

ARCHAIC, SUSA
DCL,XVI,21

F6

CRETE   M.S.III

F9

-570
NAUKRATIS
JHS 1924·XI

7

G1

-570
NAUKRATIS
JHS 1924·XI

G4

+600
NOCERA
MA.1918, 243

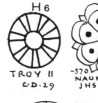

G6

+600
NOCERA, N DISK
MA 1918 343

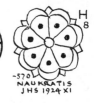

G8

COMMINGES   EG 882

H3

H4

XVIII AMARNA
P.A.XVIII

H6

TROY II
C·D.29

H8

-570
NAUKRATIS
JHS 1924·XI

H9

SASSANIAN HFD.LXV
E.TURKESTAN

8

J1

MM II
PORTI
X.M.VIII

J3

MM II KNOSSOS, EPM,194

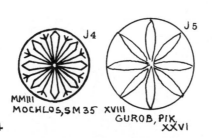

J4

MM III
MOCHLOS, SM 35

J5

XVIII
GUROB, PIK
XXVI

J6

CRETE, HS,25

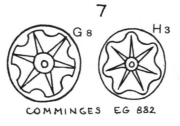

J8

RELIEF
ASHUR
ACA, p.9

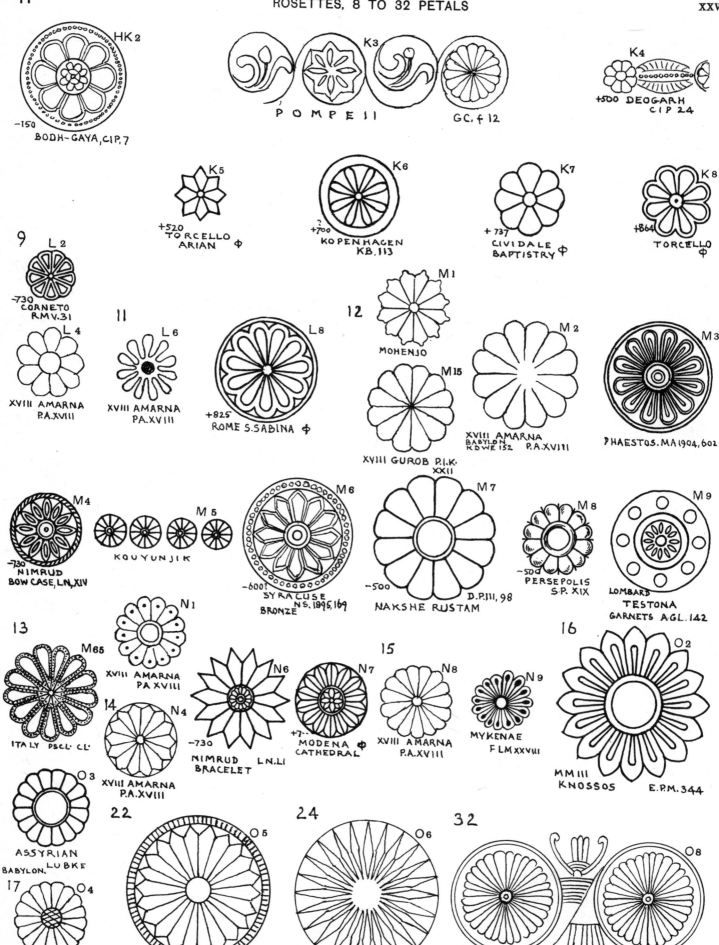

HK 2
-150
BODH-GAYA, CIP. 7

K 3
P O M P E I I
GC. f 12

K 4
+500 DEOGARH
CIP 24

K 5
+520
TORCELLO
ARIAN Φ

K 6
+700
KOPENHAGEN
KB. 113

K 7
+737
CIVIDALE
BAPTISTRY Φ

K 8
+864
TORCELLO
Φ

9
L 2
-730
CORNETO
RM V. 31

11
L 4
XVIII AMARNA
P.A. XVIII

L 6
XVIII AMARNA
PA. XVIII

L 8
+825
ROME S. SABINA Φ

12
M 1
MOHENJO

M 15
XVIII GUROB P.I.K.
XXII

M 2
XVIII AMARNA
BABYLON
KDWE 152   P.A. XVIII

M 3
PHAESTOS. MA 1904, 602

M 4
-730
NIMRUD
BOW CASE, LN. XIV

M 5
KOUYUNJIK

M 6
-600?
SYRACUSE
NS. 1895, 169
BRONZE

M 7
-500
NAKSHE RUSTAM
D.P. III, 98

M 8
-500
PERSEPOLIS
S.P. XIX

M 9
LOMBARD
TESTONA
GARNETS A.GL. 142

13
M 65
ITALY PSCL. CL.

N 1
XVIII AMARNA
PA XVIII

14
N 4
XVIII AMARNA
P.A. XVIII

15
N 6
-730
NIMRUD
BRACELET   LN. LI

N 7
+7..
MODENA Φ
CATHEDRAL

N 8
XVIII AMARNA
P.A. XVIII

N 9
MYKENAE
F LM XXVIII

16
O 2
MM III
KNOSSOS   E.P.M. 344

O 3
ASSYRIAN
BABYLON.   LUBKE

17
O 4
XVIII AMARNA
P.A. XVIII

22
O 5
LM II
MYKENAE TOMB 3   BAK 312

24
O 6
MM II
PHAESTOS, EPM, 198

32
-750 FALERII

O 8
M. I. 326. 7

JB 1

-1400 IALYSOS FLM VI
-1300? NAUPLIA FLM XV

B 3

B 5

-1400? IALYSOS, SAA 1926 f 87

B 7

L HEL. III

KORAKOU   B K 84

D 2

MYKENAE, FLM XXXII   CRETE   FLM p.23

D 6

ALYABAD, MAK 912

D 4

1400 IALYSOS
FLM VIII

D 5

SUSA II   CA. 15

D 7

LM I   MA 1903.52

D 8

DAUNIA MA P·XIII, II

D 9

-1450 IALYSOS, SAA, 1926 f 51

G 2

-650
BISENZIO   MA·1912,409
PALESTRINA MA 1905,558
VULCI   DF 380

G 3

GOLD RELIEF ON
SILVER GROUND
+? EGYPT UC

G 4

FE I
TUNISIA
DF 383

G 6

LM.I. MOCHLOS
SM XI

G 8

-570 DEFENNEH, P.D. XXVII

3   KB

M MIII   57
KNOSSOS, ABS 1903

4

C 1

MM·I   PALAIKASTRO
EPM 133

C 3

XVIII HAPUSENB   JDE. 40

C 4

PALAIKASTRO
ABS 1902, XIX

C 5

-700   CUMA
M·A·1913 xLvii

C 6

-650 EPHESOS
BASIS
HEE VI·II,14

C 7

-570
NAUKRATIS
JHS·1924·XI

C 8

SYRACUSE
MA·1918,537

C 9

+530
DRESS S. THEODORE
COSMO ET DAMIAN
W.M·107

6

D 1

GOURNIA BHG 28

D 3

-550?
OLBIA   JI·1914, 243

7

E 2

CRETE MS·XV

E 4

-700?
CUMA
M·A·1913 xLi

E 5

ITALY   PSC L·CLXXXVI

E 6

MONT·IV
U.P. BAVARIA, SAK·127

D 5

-500   ESTE   R.M·I·7·7
BENVENUTE SITULA
M MIII KNOSSOS ABS 1903 82

D 7

+1000
STROGANOFF
IVORY WSA·XXVI

D 9

+570
FAIRFORD AAS·28

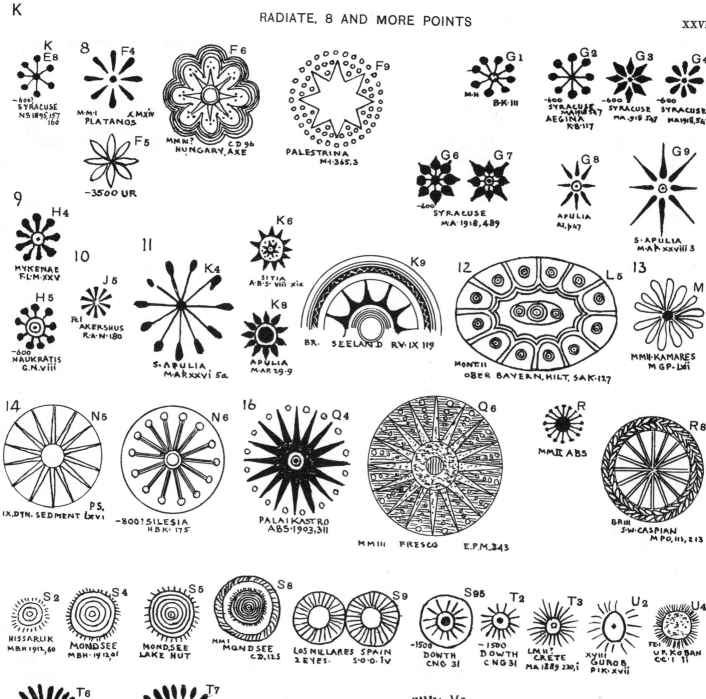

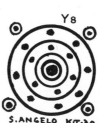

LA3

HONAN   CA·13

AZILIAN ARUDY An.1904 p.145
12 M. S. OF PAU, PYRENEES

A8   TROY 5·1·

A13   SD 31-3 AMRAH EGYPT MADP iii

A18   SD 40 NAQADEH PN B XXXIV. 33 a

A26

A23

NEO² FLOMBORN L.A.V. i

NEO² EICHELSBACH L.A.V. i.
30 M·E· OF FRANKFORT

A28   NEO² ILBENSTADT. LA·V· i

A33   ARCHAIC. SUSA. DCL. XVii, 14

A36   NEO² FLOMBORN . LA,V, i

A38   NEO² RAKHMANI, W.T. 9

A43   MM k, VASILIKI   E.P.M.134

A48   RAKHMANI NEO² WT ii

A53   EMI? SESKLO RV I viii

A58   DIMINI GREECE RAG.3 RAKHMANI, WT.13

A63   BUKOWINA. M5,93

A72   EMI? THESSALY LIANOKLADI RV·I iX

A73   EM. SYROS RV·VII· CLXXX

A83   MYKENAE FLM.XXX

A88   HITTITE H·H·136 THRACE A·ANZ,1913 347

A93   E.M·I? SESKLO. RAG.3

A68   NEO.CU. E·GALICIA·HU·II·187

A8   -1500 DOWTH CNG.36

A86   MYKENAE, F. LM XXX i

A98   -50 SANCHI C·I·P·13

B6   AZILIAN ARUDY. An.1904 137

B10   AZILIAN ARUDY An.1904, p.146

B14   NEOL. CAPITAINE LE TRAVAUX

B18   NEO.CU. E·GALICIA· HU·II·187

B22   HASBENGAU BELGIUM NEO. M·B·H,1912, 56

B26   EM·III MOCHLOS; SM,19

B30   IX DYN, PS,lvii SEDMENT

B34   CAPPADOC. G.CC.II 7651

B38   MM· PHAISTOS MSAC·I· ix Φ

B42   FALERII M·1,326.4 1400 IALYSOS F.L.M. vii

B46   FE ANANINO, VIATKA A.A.F. 467

B50   CAPPADOCIA GCC II 7651

B54   RAISAN A·A·F. 915

B66   TENE ZLONITZ BOHEMIA MF·9

B70   700? CU MA M·A·1913,XLi

B74   700? IALYSOS PITHOI, S·A·A·1926,209

B78   LENGYEL -700? CDP 283

B82   BR· KOBAN MAK·XVIII TROY SI·1889

B86   800? CUMA M·A 1913,XVii

B90   -600 NOCERA M·A·1918·164

B92   TENE III LOIRE, D.F2, 682

B58   MMII CRETE E·S·M· p,161

B62   M·M·III MOCHLOS S·M·31

B96   CAPUA   K.T.XXViii

B98   C   NEMI, TEMPLE POTy M·A·1903, 320

LC 2

NEO.
CUCUTENI S·A·E·II·xxix
Nᵣ JASSY

C 6

C 4

–2500 ERÖSD
CDP 99

E.M.II, TRANSYLVANIA CD.69

C 8

EM II TRANSYLVANIA. CD 69

C 10

L·HEL·I KORAKOU

B·K·57

C 12

L·M·I MOCHLOS, S.M.xi

C 14

CERNAVODA
SAE 8 b

C 16

NEO·CU· E·GALICIA   S·A·K· VIii,2

C 18

NEO·CU·E·GALICIA·HUII
187

C·20

NEO·CU·
SERAYEVO,H.U·II,215

C 22

–2500 ERÖSD TRANSYLV. CD.68

C 24

NEO. BUTMIR, MBH 1912
51

C 26

NEQ. BUTMIR,MBH,1912,51

C 28

NEO. BUTMIR, MBH 1912,51

C 30

NEO·CU.SERAYEVO,HU II
215

C 32

NEO.
SERAYEVO,H.U·II·215

C 34

BUTMIR   CA 23

C 36

E.M.III MOCHLOS   EPM. 76

HC44

XVIII AMENEMHAT,THEBES, J·D·E·30

C 48

LM·I HAGHIA TRIADA MA·1908,xix

C 50

LM III TIRYNS   DCP 124

C 54

STELE III
MYKENAE
ABS 1923
130

C 38

C 40

XII KAHUN. P·I·K·i   XII KAHUN,RIK·i

C 52

LM·III TRIPOLYE B., M·S·G· 32
KIEV 50N 30%E

C 46

NEO.
LENGYEL
HUNGARY
RV·VII,CCi

C42

BR· KOBAN, CAUCASUS MAK XVI

C 43

L·M·II, ALIKI,ATTICA, FLM XVIII

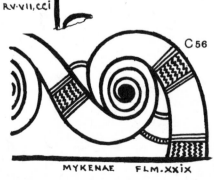

C 56

MYKENAE   FLM.XXIX

C 58

MM II. KNOSSOS EPM II ix
(AS SENUSERT II)
SEE LC 92

C 60 MM·II UKRAINE CD·7·–900?

C 62 LATRONICO, LUCANIA, M·A·1916, 494

C 64 LATRONICO, LUCANIA MA·1916 487

C 66 SEE UJ2 MMIa KNOSSOS. ABS·1905

C 68 BR·IV MAGLEBY DENMARK NF·I·XXI

C 70 L·M·III TRIPOLYE A. M·S·G·29

C 72 M·M·III MOCHLOS S·M·51

C 78 TOMSK, AAF.170

C 74 MONT·V. HANGEBEKENS SWEDEN S·A·K·XII

C 76 –700 PLEVNA BULGARIA TENE MARNE MF6 R·V·XIV·LIV

C 80 HITTITE SAE II 60

C 82 700 IALYSOS PITHOI S·A·A·1926, 221

C 84 CYLINDER U.C.

C 86 XII U.C.

C 87 XII MM·I· UC

C 88 XII MM·I· U.C.

C 89 XII MM·I· U.C.

C 90 M·M·IIIA KNOSSOS E·P·M·272

C 92 M.M. PHAESTOS M.P.C.122 SEE LC 58

C 94 BR·IV. MAGLEBY, DENMARK, NFI XXI

C 95 –800? GAURA HUNGARY R·V·IV·XCIV

C 96 MONT·V. HANGEBEKENS SWEDEN S·A·K·XII

C 98 700? IALYSOS PITHOI. S·A·A·1926, 209

C 99 ALEXANDROPOL HUGEL LOW DNEIPER R·V·XIII· XXXVI B

D 7 MMI· PLATANOS·X·M·XIII

D 35 CRETE M·S·II

D 42 LM III IALYSOS S·A·A·1926, 81

D 63 LM II KNOSSOS TAP.II 60

D 70 TENE III MURCIA D.F.2, 685

D 84 NARCE MA·1894, 234.

D 91 ETRUSCAN, LOUVRE, C·N·G·60

D 14 MMI· PLATANOS·X·M·XIII

D 49 HITTITE CYL. H.W 863

D 77 BR AK BUNAR, MACEDONIA, A, 1925, XXVII

D 97 2000–1500? NEW GRANGE M·P·I·86 C·N·G·59

D 21 MMI· KUMASA·X·MIV

D 56 L·H·II KORAKOU B·K·PL·V

D 28 CRETE, M·6·39

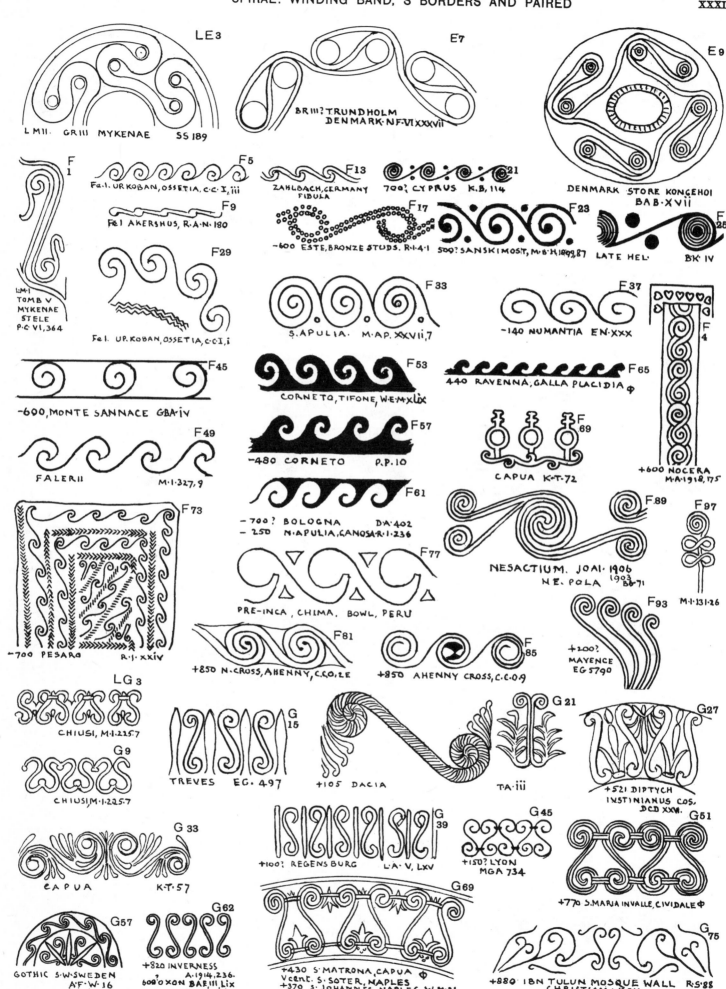

LE3

LMII. GRIII MYKENAE   SS 189

E7

BRIII? TRUNDHOLM
DENMARK. NF·VI·XXXvii

E9

DENMARK STORE KONGEHOI
BAB·XVII

F1

LM·I
TOMB V
MYKENAE
STELE
P·C·VI,364

F5

Fa·I· UR·KOBAN, OSSETIA, C·C·I,iii

F9

Fe·I· AKERSHUS, R·A·N· 180

F29

Fe·I· UR·KOBAN, OSSETIA, C·C·I,i

F13

ZAHLBACH, GERMANY
FIBULA

F17

-600 ESTE, BRONZE STUDS· R·I·4·1

F21

700? CYPRUS K·B, 114

F23

500? SANSKI MOST, M·B·H·1899,87

F25

LATE HEL·   BK· IV

F33

S. APULIA· M·AP· XXVii,7

F37

-140 NUMANTIA EN·XXX

F45

-600, MONTE SANNACE GBA·iv

F49

FALERII   M·I·327,9

F53

CORNETO, TIFONE, W·E·M·xlix

F57

-480 CORNETO   P.P.10

F61

-700? BOLOGNA   D·A·402
-250 N·APULIA, CANOSA·R·I·236

F65

440 RAVENNA, GALLA PLACIDIA Φ

F69

CAPUA K·T·72

F4

+600 NOCERA
M·A·1918,175

F73

-700 PESARO   R·J·xxiv

F77

PRE-INCA, CHIMA, BOWL, PERU

F81

+850 N·CROSS, AHENNY, C·CO·2E

F85

+850 AHENNY CROSS, C·C·O·9

F89

NESACTIUM. JOAI·1906
1903
N·E·POLA   B·671

F97

M·I·131·26

F93

+200?
MAYENCE
EG 5790

LG3

CHIUSI, M·I·225·7

G9

CHIUSI M·I·225·7

G15

TREVES   EG· 497

G21

+105 DACIA   T·A·iii

G27

+521 DIPTYCH
INSTINIANUS COS,
DCD·XXVI.

G33

CAPUA   K·T·57

G39

+100? REGENSBURG   L·A·V, LXV

G45

+150? LYON
MGA 734

G51

+770 S·MARIA INVALLE, CIVIDALE Φ

G57

GOTHIC S·W·SWEDEN
A·F·W·16

G62

+820 INVERNESS
A·1914,236.
600 OXON BAE·III,Lix

G69

+430 S·MATRONA, CAPUA Φ
Vcent. S· SOTER, NAPLES
+370 S·JOHANNES NAPLES, W·M·31

G75

+880 IBN TULUN MOSQUE WALL R·S·88
CHRISTIAN WORK

LH2
MM·I·
KALATHIANA, X·M·VIII

H3
DENMARK
M·A·K·262

H5
FE·I·
UP·KOBAN OSSETIA
C·E·I, xi

H7
TENE   MARNE   DF2.697

H8
FE·2·
SHLESVIG-HOLSTIEN
DF2, 390
SEE C B 30

H9
FE
VLADIMIR
AAF, 892

H6
-1500
NEW GRANGE
CNG 9

LJ5
UR, SHUB-AD. FP

J10
E.M. III
MESSARA, EPM.86

J15
MM·I·
KOMASA   X·M·IV

J20
KOMASA, CRETE, X·M·IV
M.M.I

J25
MM·I·
PLATANOS, X·M·XIII

J30
MM I
PHAESTOS   M·A·1905

J35
MM·I·
KNOSSOS   E·P·M·205

J40
CRETE   MS·XIV

J45
LMII
PYLOS MAIA   1909 285

J50
XI SA·KHENTI·KHATI   U.C.

J55
XI   EGYPT   U.C.

J60
XI-XII   U.C.

J65
MM·II· C·D·16
MYKENAE
DENMARK
BAB I

J75
TENE I. L·A·V, pl·50

J80
XVIII AMARNA P·A·XVIII

J85
MONT·V.   BAVARIA
S·A·K·127

J90
-50 SANCHI
C·I·P·13

J95
MM·I·
TROY C·D·29

LK1
FE-I   LOWER AUSTRIA   H·U·II· 223

K4
L·M·ii   MYKENAE GR·III, S·S·169

K5
MYKENAE·MS·C·I·XIV

K7
(I)
MALTA DC·P. 150

K72
MALTA, SHRINE A·LXVIII
xxxiv

K2
FE·I· LOWER AUSTRIA   H·U·II·224

K3
DONETZ   C·D·86

K44
L·M·ii   MYKENAE, GR·III·S·S·170

K6
-1300 MYKENAE
ABS 1923 381

K8
MM·I· XUMASA, X·M·V

K9
BR.
AKERSHUS, RAN.
1251

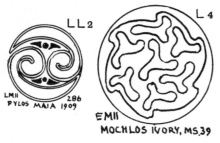

LL 2
LM II 286
PYLOS MAIA 1909

L 4
EM II
MOCHLOS IVORY, MS.39

L 5
MMI
PLATANOS
X·M·Xiii

L 7
MMI
PLATANOS
X·M·Xiii

L 9
LM I
MYKENAE GR·IV, S·S·229

M 2
PERTOSA, M.A.1916,594

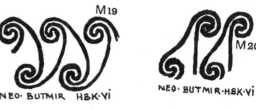

M 19
NEO· BUTMIR HBK·VI

M 20
NEO· BUTMIR·HBK·VI

M 4
M.A 1899,583
SALERNO, CAVE

M 7
V DYN, ASSA U.C.

M 13
IX DYN P.S.Lvii
SEDMENT

M 16
X DYN, P.S.Lvii
SEDMENT

M 29
EM·III KAMARES EPM.77

M 32
EM III CDii CRETE
H.TRIADA,THOLOS

M 37
EM II CRETE, M·S·XII

M 40
XII LAHUN P.I.K.X,144

M 43
M.M.I, XM viii
PORTI, CRETE

M 46
MM.I,XMXiii PLATA·NOS

M 48
XI? U.C. EGYPT

M 52
XII U.C. EGYPT

M 55
XII P.I.K.X·176 EGYPT

M 57
XII MMI-II, U.C. EGYPT

M 64
LM II
PYLOS MAIA 1909.284

M 67
-1050 GR.V. MYKENAE S.S.145

M 68
FE·I LANGELEBARN LOWER AUSTRIA CA·20

M 73
XVIII EGYPT U.C.

M 76
-650? EPHESOS BASIS HEE·VIII 27

M 79
M 82
FE·I. W.NORWAY RAN 294

M 88
CRETE AJA.1897,259

M 83 M 87
-650? EPHESOS BASIS HEE·IX·47
EPHESOS WEST HEE·IX·46

M 92
EPHESOS -650 BASIS HEE VIII 25

M 93
-650? EPHESOS BASIS HEE·IV 31

M 94
-650? EPHESOS BASIS HEE·VIII 29

M 96
700 CRETE K·B·114

M 97
-1800? HUNGARY CDP.270

L N 3
Relief
BUTMIR
M.B.H. 1912
49

N 7
BUTMIR
CA 23

N 11
Incised
BUTMIR M.B.H. 1912, 50

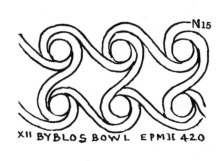

N 15
XII BYBLOS BOWL EPMII 420

N 19
XVIII, L·M·II AMARNA   P.A. X

N 23
KAMEIROS
SINGLE LINE · ABS·1906,72

N 27
-700? IALYSOS PITHOI   S·A·A·1926, 210
SYRO-HITTITE CYLINDERS, HW855-7
-650 CRETE MAIA 1906, xxiii

N 31
L·M·I   PSEIRA   B·A·K·167

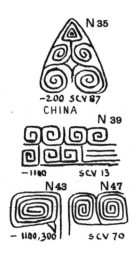

N 35
-200 SCV87
CHINA

N 39
-1180   SCV 13

N 43   N 47
-1100, 300   SCV 70

N 51
XIX L·M·III   NESI·PA·NEFER·HETEP, J·D·E· 51

N 55
206
L·M·II ORCHOMENOS B·A·K

N 59
MMI·SPHOUNGARAS
MGP L·ix

N 63
MMI·SPHOUNGARAS
MGP J· L·ix

N 67
ORKNEY BOX
ACM p. xcviii

N 71
-480 BIRKENFELD
RV·VII·CXCi
SEE GQ 6, 7. LXXXVII 82

N 75
FE·2·   BIRKENFELD, MOSELLE DF2· 695

N 79
KAKOVATOS·A·M·1909,xii

N 83
FE·I· WALDALGESHEIM, B·M·C·E

N 87
-750   ESTE   N·S·1882 iv
SYRO-HITTITE CYL· HW·898
-650 CRETE MAIA 1906 xxiii

N 91
X CENT. GRAIGUE NAMANACH
C·C·O·13

LO

THESSALY
NEO² RAKHMANI WT. i

O9

GOZO, GIGANTEIA ETP. 68

O14

BARANYA, HUNGARY   S·A·26

O19

TARXIEN A. 1916, XXii

O24

TARXIEN, A. 1916, XVI

O29

MALTA SHRINE φ
A·LXVIII, XXXIV

O34

MALTA, BENCH, A. LXVIII, XXXVII

O39

TARXIEN, A. 1916 XVI

O44

TARXIEN   A. 1916, XXI

O49

CRETE   MA· 1895 IX

O54

MALTA   A·LXVIII, 282

O64

MORITZING, TYROL
B. C. 77

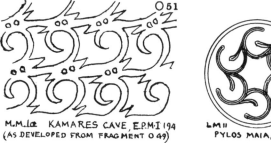

O51

M.M.I☾ KAMARES CAVE, E.P.M·I 194
(AS DEVELOPED FROM FRAGMENT O 49)

O59

LM II
PYLOS MAIA, 1909, 283

O69

MALTA, BENCH, A. LXVIII, XXXVII

O71

DRESS, HAGHIA TRIADA MA 1903 X

O79

MALTA, BENCH, A. LXVIII, XXXI φ
= A. 1916 XXII

O84

TARXIEN
A 1916 XXII

O74

MALTA BOWL   A. LXVIII, 280

C89

MALTA BENCH   A. LXVIII, XXXVII φ

O94

TARXIEN A. 1914 XXI

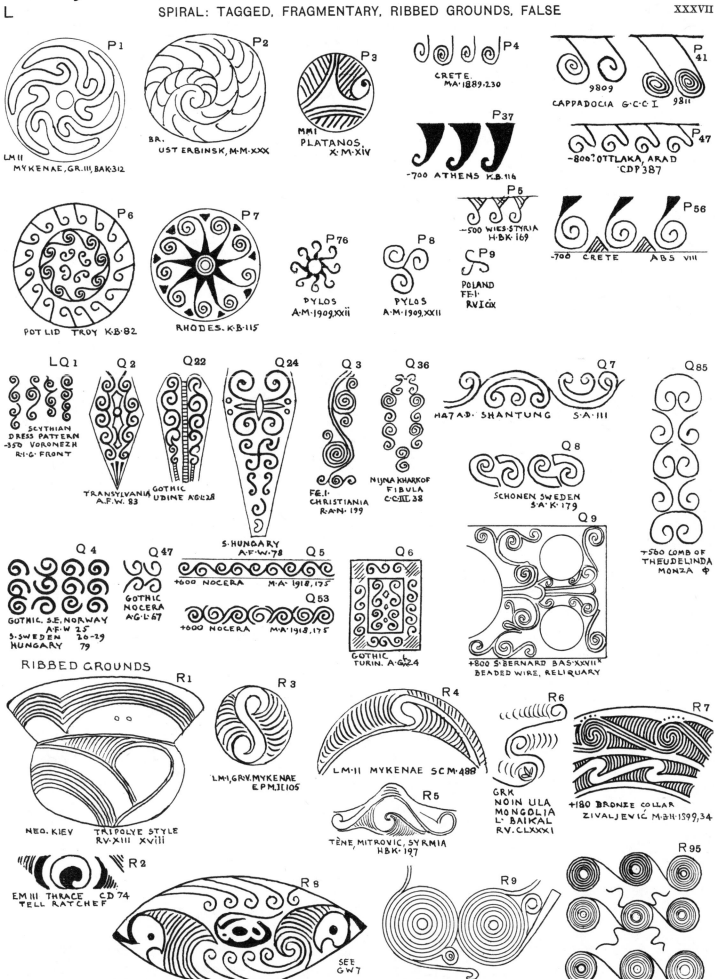

P1 LM II MYKENAE, GR.III, BAK·312

P2 BR. UST ERBINSK, M·M·XXX

P3 MMI PLATANOS X·M·XIV

P4 CRETE. M·A·1889·230

P41 9809 CAPPADOCIA G·C·C·I 9811

P37 -700 ATHENS K·B·116

P47 -800? OTTLAKA, ARAD CDP 387

P6 POT LID TROY K·B·82

P7 RHODES. K·B·115

P76 PYLOS A·M·1909·XXII

P8 PYLOS A·M·1909·XXII

P9 POLAND FE·I· R·V·I cix

P5 -500 WIES·STYRIA H·BK·169

P56 -700 CRETE ABS VIII

LQ1 SCYTHIAN DRESS PATTERN -350 VORONEZH R·I·G· FRONT

Q2 TRANSYLVANIA A·F·W· 83

Q22 GOTHIC UDINE A·G·L·28

Q24 S. HUNGARY A·F·W·78

Q3 FE·I· CHRISTIANIA R·A·N· 199

Q36 NIJNA KHARKOF FIBULA C·C·III· 38

Q7 H47 A·D· SHANTUNG S·A·III

Q85 +560 COMB OF THEUDELINDA MONZA φ

Q8 SCHONEN SWEDEN S·A·K· 179

Q9 +800 S· BERNARD BAS XXVII BEADED WIRE, RELIQUARY

Q4 GOTHIC. S.E. NORWAY A·F·W 25 S. SWEDEN 26-29 HUNGARY 79

Q47 GOTHIC NOCERA A·G·L· 67

Q5 +600 NOCERA M·A·1918,175

Q53 +600 NOCERA M·A·1918,175

Q6 GOTHIC TURIN. A·G·24

RIBBED GROUNDS

R1 NEO. KIEV TRIPOLYE STYLE R·V·XIII xviii

R3 LM·I, GR·V, MYKENAE E·P·M·III·105

R4 LM·II MYKENAE SCM·488

R5 TÈNE, MITROVIC, SYRMIA H·BK·197

R6 GRK NOIN ULA MONGOLIA L· BAIKAL R·V· CLXXXI

R7 +180 BRONZE COLLAR ZIVALJEVIĆ M·B·H·1899,34

R2 EM III THRACE CD 74 TELL RATCHEF

R8 + -25 TO +220 CHINA S·A·C· XXIV SEE GW7

R9 L·M·II MYKENAE, GR·III, S·S·191

R95 -1000 BOLOGNA R·M·V· 4

LS

S 3

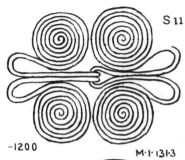

S 7

S 11

MM. KYTHERA STEATITE. M·S·40
EP M II 117 B

−500 NAKSHE RUSTAM DP III 92

−1200

M·I·131·3

S 16

S 19

S 27

S 31

S 36

S 41

ZENJIRLI
SHIR·123

XII.? PBS vii 73
EGYPT

LMH·GR·V, MYKENAE
SS 145

C·CROSS
CASTLE DERMOT
C·C·O·1

BR III SW·CASPIAN
M·P·O·III·2·13

L·M·I
TOMB V MYKENAE, SS·274

S 56

S 61

S 81

S 46

SEE F H, 1, 2

FRANK. VAUD, AFW·168

+850 AHENNY. C·C·O·XIVA

HALTON OF CADBOLL SSS·XXV

CAHIR LEHILLAN C·C·O
J 9

S 52

S 66

S 71

S 91

CLONFERT, C·C·O·3 C

LIND ISFARN
+700 MLG 27

+924 MUIRDACH. MONASTERBOICE.

+800 CAVAN   A·1914 xxvii

LT

T 1

T 16

T 2

T 3

SYRO CAPPADOC, AIDIN
DCL. XCVI, 24

U·P·KOBAN
OSSETIA
C·C·I·ii

PRAG   S·A·K·VIII·1

SCANDINAVIAN AXE, CD 102

T 59

T 6

T 7

T 5

+770 ELY   A·1915, 236

KINITTY CROSS   C·C·O·3 G

+850 AHENNY
C·C·O 15

T 4

ILKLEY
BEO 59

DACRE
BEO. 42

T 8

−1350 MYKENAE
AB5 1923, 107

T 9

+450 FRILFORD
A·A·S·19

T 95

+450 OXON·A·A·S·18

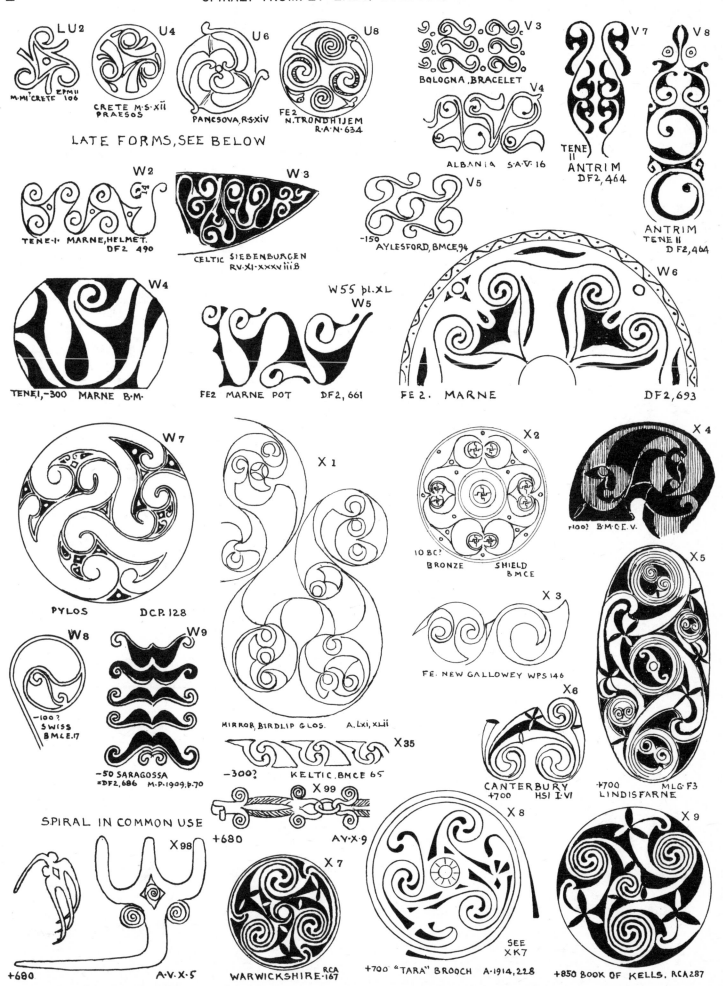

LU2 M.MI'CRETE RPMII 106

U4 CRETE M.S.xii PRAESOS

U6 PANCSOVA, R.S.xiv

U8 FE2 N.TRONDHIJEM R.A.N.634

V.3 BOLOGNA, BRACELET

V4

V 7 TENE II ANTRIM DF2, 464

V 8 ANTRIM TENE II DF2, 464

LATE FORMS, SEE BELOW

ALBANIA S.A.V. 16

W2 TENE·I· MARNE, HELMET. DF2 490

W3 CELTIC SIEBENBURGEN RV·XI·xxxviiiB

V5 -150 AYLESFORD, BMCE.94

W4 TENEI,-300 MARNE B.M.

W55 pl.XL W5 FE2 MARNE POT DF2, 661

W 6

FE 2. MARNE DF2,693

W 7 PYLOS DCP. 128

X 1

X 2 10 BC? BRONZE SHIELD BMCE

X 4 +100? B·M·C·E·V.

X 5

X 3 FE. NEW GALLOWEY WPS 146

W8 -100? SWISS BMCE.17

W9 -50 SARAGOSSA =DF2,686 M·P·1909,p·70

MIRROR, BIRDLIP GLOS. A.Lxi,xLii

X35 -300? KELTIC. BMCE 65

X 99 +680 A·V·X·9

X 6 CANTERBURY +700 HSI I·VI

+700 MLG·F3 LINDISFARNE

SPIRAL IN COMMON USE

X 98 +680 A·V·X·5

X 7 WARWICKSHIRE·167 RCA

X 8 +700 "TARA" BROOCH A·1914,228 SEE XK7

X 9 +850 BOOK OF KELLS. RCA287

Y2

FE2. NORWAY
R·A·N·635

Y25

FE STICHEL W.P.S.121

Y3

KIRKCUD BRIGHT
BR·ARM·WPS·132

Y35

LINZ   MUS.
R·S·xiii,1

Y40

LINZ MUS R·S·xiii,11

Y43

LINZ MUS.
R·S·xiii 1,4

Y47

KLAUSENBERG MUS.R·S·XIV,2

Y5

+100? IRELAND
BMCE 144

Y7

GOTHIC BOHEMIA
A·F·W·18

Y8

COPTIC CHURCH, OLD CAIRO, R·S·87

Y60

BROOCH
JS H·161. WILDE CATAL.

Y64

STOKESTOWN

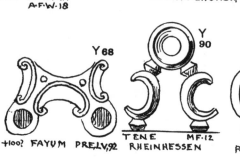

Y67

WALTERS
HIST·ANC·POTT
204

Y68

+100? FAYUM PRE.LV,92

Y90

TENE   MF.12
RHEINHESSEN

Y96

MODERN
LOUIS QUINZE

RACIAL REVIVAL
OF C BLOBS

Z2

BR. LOCHAR MOSS TORC   W.P.S ix

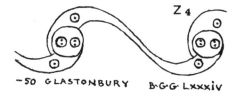

Z4

-50 GLASTONBURY   B·G·G·Lxxxiv

Z5

-50 GLASTONBURY.   B·G·G·Lxxiii

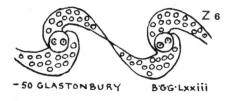

Z6

-50 GLASTONBURY   B·G·G·Lxxiii

Z7

+100
PORTLAND   DORSET 127   BMCE

Z8

-50 GLASTONBURY   B·G·G· LXXi

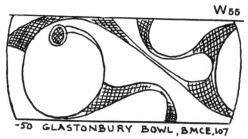

W55

-50 GLASTONBURY BOWL, BMCE,107

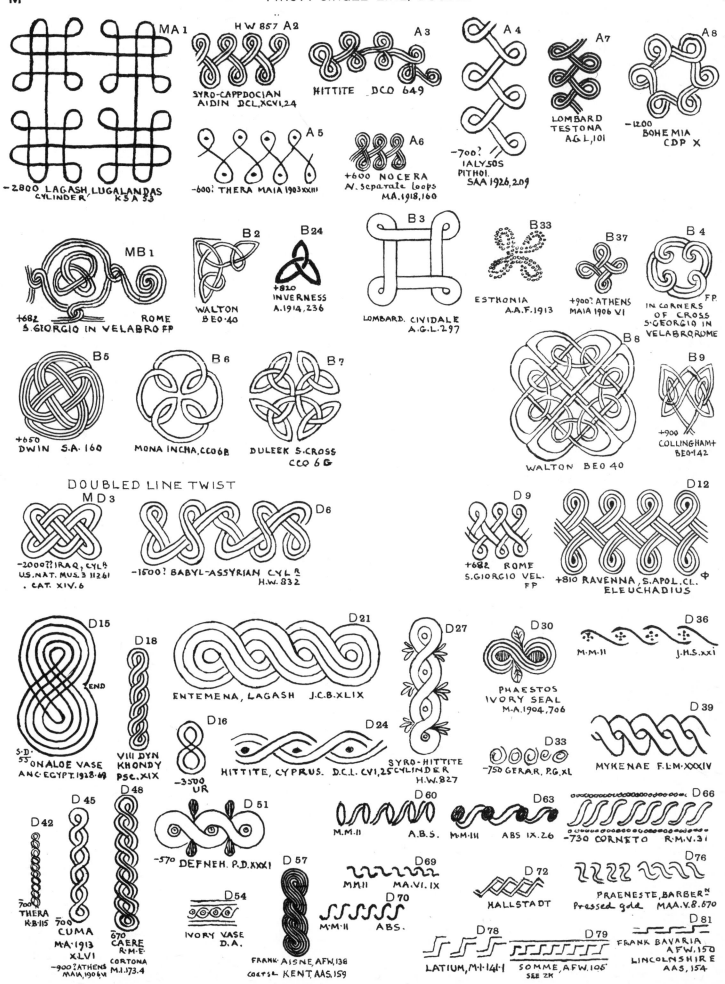

MA 1
−2800 LAGASH LUGALANDAS 'CYLINDER' K.S.A.53

H W 857 A2
SYRO-CAPPDOCIAN AIDIN DCL.XCVI.24

A3
HITTITE DCO 649

A4
−700? IALYSOS PITHOI. SAA 1926,209

A7
LOMBARD TESTONA A.G.L.101

A8
−1200 BOHEMIA CDP X

A5
−600? THERA MAIA 1903 XXIII

A6
+600 NOCERA N. Separate loops MA.1918,160

MB 1
+682 ROME S.GIORGIO IN VELABRO FP

B 2
WALTON BEO.40

B24
+820 INVERNESS A.1914,236

B3
LOMBARD. CIVIDALE A.G.L.297

B33
ESTHONIA A.A.F.1913

B37
+900? ATHENS MAIA 1906 VI

B4
IN CORNERS OF CROSS S·GEORGIO IN VELABRO ROME FP.

B5
+650 DWIN S.A.160

B6
MONA INCHA,CCO6B

B7
DULEEK S.CROSS CCO 6 G

B8
WALTON BEO 40

B9
+900 COLLINGHAM+ BEO·142

DOUBLED LINE TWIST
MD 3
−2000?? IRAQ, CYLR US.NAT. MUS.3 11261 . CAT. XIV.6

D6
−1500? BABYL-ASSYRIAN CYLR H.W. 832

D 9
+682 ROME S.GIORGIO VEL. FP

D 12
+810 RAVENNA, S.APOL.CL. ELEUCHADIUS

D15
S·D· 55 ONALOE VASE ANC EGYPT. 1928·67

D 18
VIII DYN KHONDY PSC.XIX

D 21
ENTEMENA, LAGASH J.C.B.XLIX

D 27

D 30
PHAESTOS IVORY SEAL M·A·1904,706

D 36
M·M·II J.H.S.xxi

D 16
−3500 UR

D 24
SYRO-HITTITE CYLINDER H.W.827

HITTITE, CYPRUS. D.C.L. CVI,25

D 33
−750 GERAR. P.G.XL

D 39
MYKENAE F.I.M.XXXIV

D 42
−700 THERA K·B·115

D 45
700 CUMA M·A·1913 XLVI −900? ATHENS MAIA 1906VI

D 48
670 CAERE R·M·E CORTONA M.I.173.4

D 51
−570 DEFNEH. P.D.XXXI

D 54
IVORY VASE D.A.

D 57
FRANK.AISNE.AFW.138 COGESL KENT, AAS.159

D 60
M·M·II A.B.S.

D 63
M·M·III ABS IX.26

D 66
−730 CORNETO R.M.V.31

D 69
M·M·II MA.VI.IX

D 70
M·M·II ABS.

D 72
HALLSTADT

D 76
PRAENESTE,BARBERⁿ Pressed gold MAA.V.8.670

D 78
LATIUM, M·I·141·1

D 79
SOMME, AFW.105 SEE ZK

D 81
FRANK BAVARIA AFW.150 LINCOLNSHIRE AAS,154

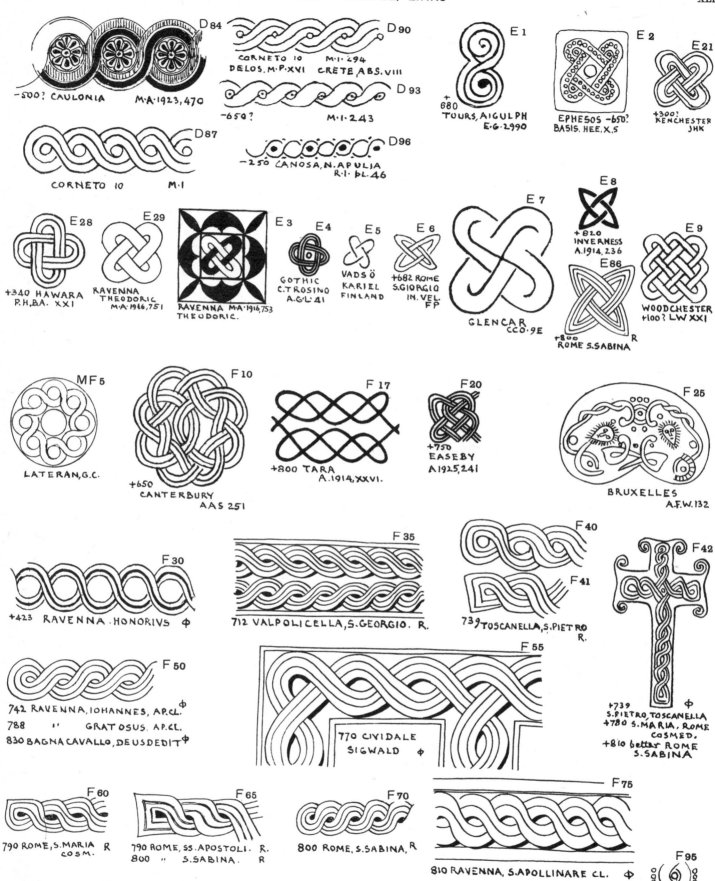

D 84   -500? CAULONIA   M·A·1923,470

D 90   CORNETO 10   M·I·294   DELOS, M·P·XVI   CRETE ABS. VIII

D 93   -650?   M·I·243

D 87   CORNETO 10   M·I

D 96   -250 CANOSA, N. APULIA   R·I· PL.46

E 1   +680 TOURS, AIGULPH   E·G·2990

E 2   EPHESOS -650?   BASIS. HEE, X.5

E 21   +300? KENCHESTER JHK

E 28   +340 HAWARA P.H.BA. XXI

E 29   RAVENNA THEODORIC M·A·1916,751

RAVENNA M·A·1916,753 THEODORIC.

E 3   GOTHIC C.TROSINO A.G·L· 41

E 4

E 5   VADSÖ KARIEL FINLAND

E 6   +682 ROME S.GIORGIO IN. VEL. FP

E 7   GLENCAR CCO·9E

E 8   +820 INVERNESS A.1914, 236

E 86   +800 ROME S.SABINA

E 9   WOODCHESTER +100? LW XXI

MF 5   LATERAN, G.C.

F 10   +650 CANTERBURY AAS 251

F 17   +800 TARA A.1914, XXVI.

F 20   +750 EASEBY A 1925,241

F 25   BRUXELLES A.F.W.132

F 30   +423 RAVENNA. HONORIVS Φ

F 35   712 VALPOLICELLA, S.GEORGIO. R.

F 40

F 41   739 TOSCANELLA, S.PIETRO R.

F 42   +739 S.PIETRO, TOSCANELLA +780 S.MARIA. ROME COSMED. +810 better ROME S.SABINA

F 50   742 RAVENNA, IOHANNES, AP.CL. Φ   788 " GRATOSUS. AP.CL.   830 BAGNACAVALLO, DEUSDEDIT Φ

F 55   770 CIVIDALE SIGWALD Φ

F 60   790 ROME, S.MARIA COSM. R

F 65   790 ROME, SS.APOSTOLI. R.   800 " S.SABINA. R

F 70   800 ROME, S.SABINA, R

F 75   810 RAVENNA, S.APOLLINARE CL. Φ

F 80   810 RAVENNA, S. APOL.CL. ELEUCHADIUS Φ

F 85   825 ROME S.SABINA Φ

F 89   +1032 MONTE FIASCONE R

F 95   BENIN ESA

M G 2

HITTITE CYLINDER. H.W.2084
SYRO—with shots in spaces H.W. 854
+500 ATHENS. S.A. 68

G 7

–700?
ARCEVIA M·I·154,4
MONTE FORTINO DF2,488
HELMET

G 12

–700? CUMA. M.A. 1913, xxxix.

G 17

GOTHIC S.W. SWEDEN
A.F.W. 16

G 22

POMPEII   G.C. fig 8

G 27

+680   A.V. XXVII, 10

G 32

M.M.III KNOSSOS EPMI, 26a

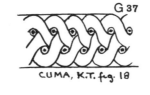

G 37

CUMA, K.T. fig. 18

G 43

MONTE CALVARIO, N.S. 1905, 232, 25

G 47

–600? SYRACUSE, MA 1918 675

G 52

–600 SYRACUSE, MA, 1918, 554

G 57

SYRACUSE M.A. 1903, XIX OLYMPEION
KALYDON P.K. XXVI.
blain centres ST. ANGELO. TA. fig 27

G 62

–450 TODI
MA 1916, 859
SYRACUSE, MA 1918, 500

G 67

–40 ROME. BAS. AEMILIA
G.A. b

G 72

POMPEII G.C. fig 12
+400–500. RAVENNA. MA 1916. 751

G 77

+191 IS–SANAMEN BSA, 5. plxix

G 82

+980?? TORCELLO PULPIT   φ

G 92

+875 TORCELLO DUOMO   φ

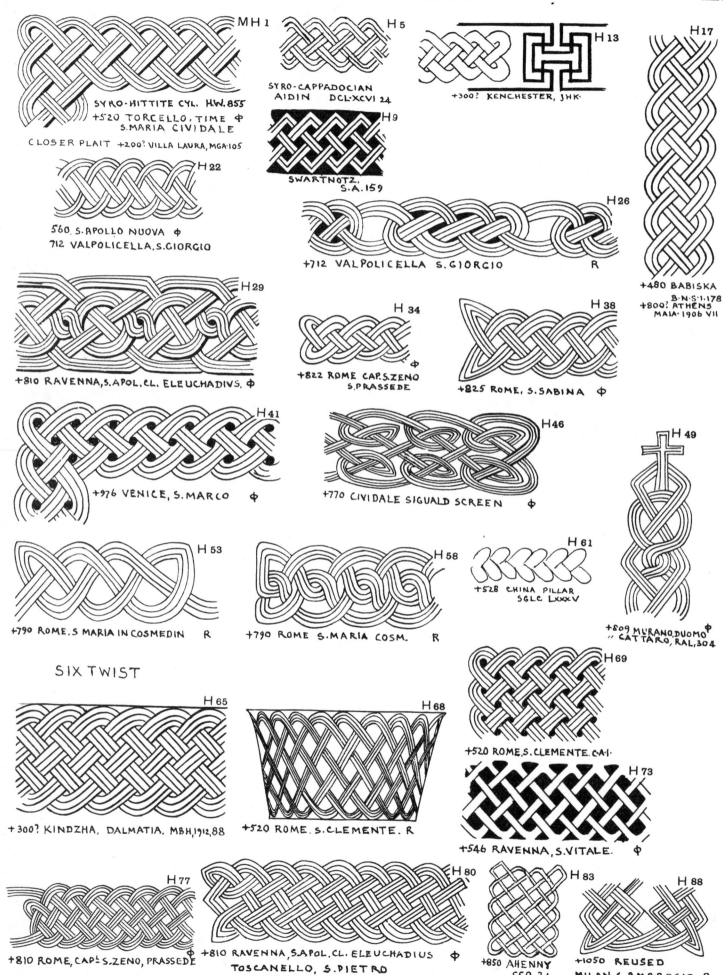

MH 1

SYRO-HITTITE CYL. H.W. 855
+520 TORCELLO, TIME Φ
S. MARIA CIVIDALE
CLOSER PLAIT +200? VILLA LAURA, MGA·105

H 5

SYRO-CAPPADOCIAN
AIDIN   DCL·XCVI 24

H 9

SWARTNOTZ.
S.A. 159

H 13

+300? KENCHESTER, JHK·

H 17

+480 BABISKA
B·N·S·I·178
+800? ATHENS
MAIA· 1906 VII

H 22

560. S. APOLLO NUOVA   Φ
712 VALPOLICELLA, S. GIORGIO

H 26

+712 VALPOLICELLA S. GIORGIO   R

H 29

+810 RAVENNA, S. APOL. CL. ELEUCHADIVS, Φ

H 34

+822 ROME CAP. S. ZENO
S. PRASSEDE

H 38

+825 ROME, S. SABINA   Φ

H 41

+976 VENICE, S. MARCO   Φ

H 46

+770 CIVIDALE SIGUALD SCREEN   Φ

H 49

+809 MURANO, DUOMO Φ
" CATTARO, RAL, 304

H 53

+790 ROME, S MARIA IN COSMEDIN   R

H 58

+790 ROME S. MARIA COSM.   R

H 61

+528 CHINA PILLAR
SGLC LXXXV

H 69

+520 ROME, S. CLEMENTE. CA·I·

SIX TWIST

H 65

+300? KINDZHA, DALMATIA. MBH,1912,88

H 68

+520 ROME. S. CLEMENTE. R

H 73

+546 RAVENNA, S. VITALE.   Φ

H 77

+810 ROME, CAP· S. ZENO, PRASSEDE

H 80

+810 RAVENNA, S. APOL. CL. ELEUCHADIUS   Φ
TOSCANELLO, S. PIETRO

H 83

+850 AHENNY
CCO 34

H 88

+1050 REUSED
MILAN, S. AMBROGIO   R

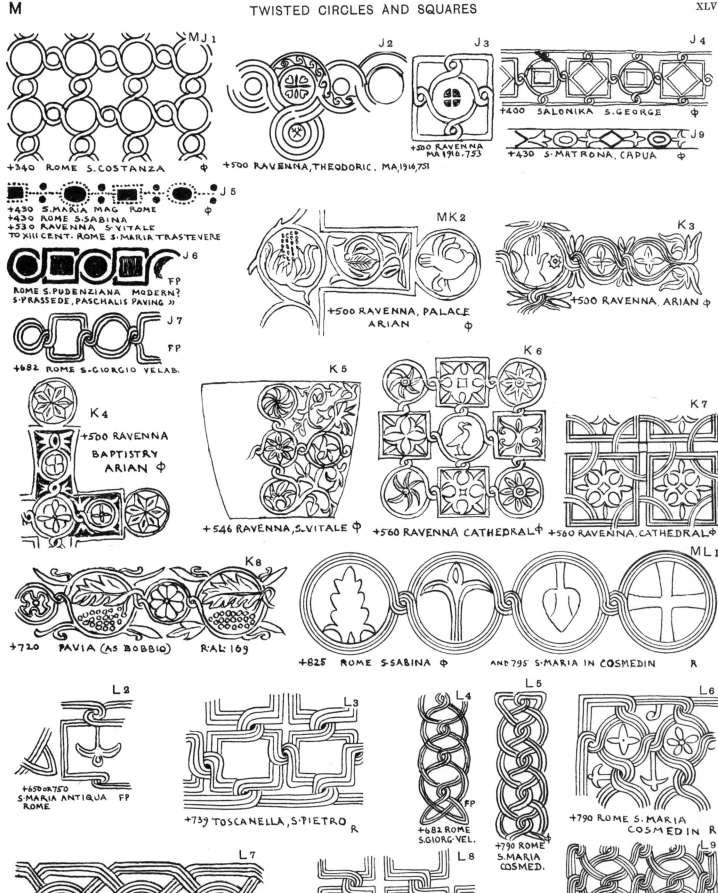

MJ1
+340 ROME S. COSTANZA   φ

J2
+500 RAVENNA, THEODORIC. MA, 1916, 751

J3
+500 RAVENNA MA 1916, 753

J4
+400 SALONIKA S. GEORGE   φ

J9
+430 S. MATRONA, CAPUA   φ

J5
+430 S. MARIA MAG ROME   φ
+430 ROME S. SABINA
+530 RAVENNA S. VITALE
TO XIII CENT. ROME S. MARIA TRASTEVERE

MK2
+500 RAVENNA, PALACE ARIAN   φ

K3
+500 RAVENNA. ARIAN   φ

J6
FP
ROME S. PUDENZIANA MODERN?
S. PRASSEDE, PASCHALIS PAVING »

J7
FP
+682 ROME S. GIORGIO VELAB.

K4
+500 RAVENNA BAPTISTRY ARIAN   φ

K5
+546 RAVENNA, S. VITALE   φ

K6
+560 RAVENNA CATHEDRAL φ

K7
+560 RAVENNA. CATHEDRAL φ

K8
+720   PAVIA (AS BOBBIO)   R. AL: 169

ML1
+825   ROME S. SABINA   φ   AND 795 S. MARIA IN COSMEDIN   R

L2
+650 OR 750
S. MARIA ANTIQUA   FP
ROME

L3
+739 TOSCANELLA, S. PIETRO   R

L4
+682 ROME
S. GIORG. VEL.   FP

L5
+790 ROME
S. MARIA
COSMED.

L6
+790 ROME S. MARIA
COSMEDIN R

L7
+810 RAVENNA   S. APOL. IN CLASSE   φ

L8
+880 MILAN, S. AMBROGIO
+1050 REUSED   R

L9
+880 MILAN. S. AMBROGIO   R
reused in 1050

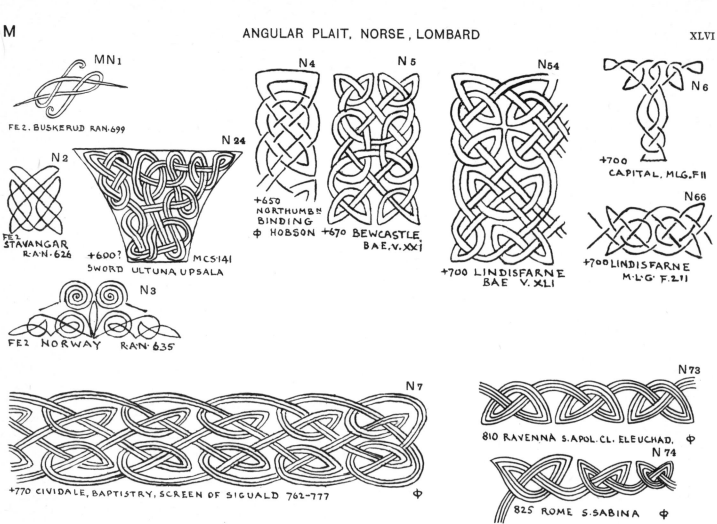

MN₁

FE 2. BUSKERUD RAN·699

N 2

FE 2 STAVANGAR R·A·N·626

N 24

+600? SWORD ULTUNA UPSALA   MCS·141

N 3

FE 2 NORWAY   R·A·N·635

N 4

+650 NORTHUMB.ᴺ BINDING ɸ HOBSON

N 5

+670 BEWCASTLE BAE.V.XXI

N 54

+700 LINDISFARNE BAE V. XLI

N 6

+700 CAPITAL, MLG.FII

N 66

+700 LINDISFARNE M·L·G· F.211

N 7

+770 CIVIDALE, BAPTISTRY, SCREEN OF SIGUALD 762-777   ɸ

N 73

810 RAVENNA S.APOL.CL. ELEUCHAD,   ɸ

N 74

825 ROME S.SABINA   ɸ

N 79

810 RAVENNA S.AP.CL. ELEUCHAD.   ɸ
840 BOLOGNA. LUDOVICUS ET LOTHARIUS CROSS. ɸ

N 9

BEALIN   C.C.O.39

MO2

+825 ROME S.SABINA   ɸ

O 3

+880 MILAN S.AMBROGIO reused 1050   R

O 4
880 MILAN S.AMBROGIO reused 1050 R

and MONASTERBOICE MUIREDACH'S CROSS +924   ɸ

O 5

+880 MILAN S.AMBROGIO columns reused 1050   R

O 6

MILAN, S.AMBROGIO   ɸ

O 7

MILAN S.AMBROGIO   R.

O 8
1132 PAVIA S.PIETRO

AND S.MICHELE +1120

MP1   TENEI ARDENNES DF2.524

P2   GARNETS. LOMBARD CIVIDALE AGL.125 OXON.AAS.165

P4   +770 ELY   A.1915,236

P5   ILKLEY BEO 50

P6   +900 COLLINGHAM+ BEO 142

P7   +900? COLLINGHAM+ BEO. 142

Q1   +600 NOCERA UMBRA M·A·1918, 267

Q2   BERKS AAS.23

Q3   +700 TARA BROOCH A·1914.228

P8   +700 LINDISFARNE B.A.E V,XXXIV

Q4   +700 LINDISFARNE B.A.E.V, XXXVII.

Q5   LEVISHAM BEO 151

Q6   YORK   BEO·155

Q7   +800 WITHAM A·1925,242

Q8   UPPLAND SWEDEN SAK. 193

Q84   +680   AV.XLI.2

Q9   +800 ST.MORITZ RELIQUARY, B·A·S·XXV

Q94   +1000 ARDRE, GOTLAND NSO 116

R1   HITTITE   D.C.O.649

R4   +680 A.V.III.6

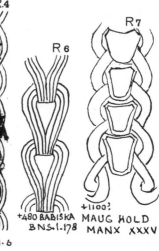
R6   +480 BABISKA BNS.I.178

R7   +1100? MAUG HOLD MANX XXXV

R3   +100? TRIER, MOSAIC G.M.19

U2   +680   AV. I.4

U3   +680   AV. I.3

U4   +680   A.V. VIII,6

U5   +680   A.V. VIII.8

U6   HÄWEENMA FINLAND AAF 1597 SIM. GETA, ALAND IS AAF 1723

U7   850 AHENNY N.CROSS   C.E·O·5A

U8   924 MONASTERBOICE, MUIREDACH, CCO 5C

A 2 — ABYDOS P.R.T.I.XXVI 1ST

A 4 — VI KOPTOS P.K.P.V

B 2 — XII KAHUN PKG XXVII 182

B 3 — -570 NAUKRATIS JHS 1924 XI

B 4 — -750 ESTE, N.S.1882 iv (ALSO SIX POINTS)

B 44 — -700 CUMA MA 1913 XLVII

B 52 — -700? ANOPOLIS J.I.1899.41

B 58 — M.I.143.5

A 6 — VII DENDERAH P.D.N.ix

A 8 — R9 ATHRIBIS P.A.T.XXI

B 23 — CAPPADOC. GCC.I.10043 MMII

B 32 — KNOSSOS EPM.186

B 59 — E.B. LOPITHOI BAB DENMARK.XXV

B 61 — APULIA MAP.29.5

B 62 — SPARTA FIBULA ABS.1907,84

B 70 — PEUKETIA M.AP.XXII.3

B 71 — -550 VALENZANO G.BA.X.1

B 74 — ASCOLI SATRIANO -550? RMI XLii.3

B 80 — APULIA MAP.29.1

B 84 — LOMBARD NOCERA GARNET AGL.130

B 9 — LOMBARD PICENO AGL.201

B 92 — +500 MITCHAM BAE.III Lvii

B 94 — +580 FAIRFORD BAE.III Lvii

B 98 — +800 SPALATO.GCK.14

FEATHERS

SCALES

F 2 — MMIII EPM.401 B

F 4 — MMIII MYKENAE EPM.401

F 8 — EARLY XVIII ΛΟΗΗΕΤΕΡ WING EPM.402

S 1 — MOHENJO-DARO

S 13 — MM.III ROBE EPM II 456

S 14 — LM.II MYKENAE GR VI FLT.XI

S 2 — XVIII AMARNA PA.X

S 23 — -1450 IALYSOS SAA.1926,f52

S 3 — -1400 IALYSOS FLM.X

S 4 — LATE HEL. KORAKOU BK.IV

S 48 — -570 DEFNEH PD.XXXII

S 53 — ±0 SCY 45

S 59 — MID APULIA M.AP.XX 4

S 91 — MODERN GRATING.JEHOL BCA.XX

S 64 — VULCI PROTOCORINT.

S 68 — M.I.264

S 76 — POMPEII B.P.

S 97 — +500 RAVENNA,MA.1916.IV THEODORIC

OB1   B2   B3   B4   B5   B6   B7   B8   B9

CRETE MS..   CRETE M·S·11   HITTITE HH·127   CILICIA PBS IV   EGYPT. PBS 225   EGYPT PBS223   EGYPT PBS 221   EGYPT PBS222   EGYPT PBS228

OC1   C2   C3   C7   C8   C9   OD1

CRETE, MS III   BOLOGNA ·1000 M·1·75   BRONZ OPEN WORK CORNETO M1·28817   TARXIEN A·1916·XVIII   TARXIEN A·1916·XVIII   MMI PORTI XM VIII   -700? KNOSSOS, J·I·1899·99

D2   D4   D7   D8   D9

-650 FEI KOBAN OSSETIA C.C. L·XXXIV   N·APULIA MAP·XVIII·3   INCHAGOIL CCO 8A   KILFENORA CCO 8B   LIVONIA AAF 2095

OE1   E3   E4   OF2   F3

MM III MYKENAE GR·III·SS·153   -1500 MC·4·12   CUMA   KT·f19   -650 ESTE M A·VII·21   -200 +250 CHINA SAC VI

E5   E6

N·APULIA MAP·XVIII·10   N·APULIA MAP·XVIII·7

F4   F7

NIMRUD BOTTA,XX, XV BALDRIC STUDDED LEATHER? ·LXXXIII   CHINA -250 SCV,121

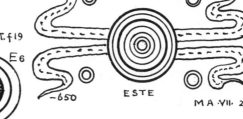

E8   E9   F8   F9

MM III, PAPUDA, CRETE EPM·341   -700 IALYSOS PITHOI SAA 1926,210   -670 CUMA RI·57   KHARKOF CC·III·37

OG   G2   G5   F5   G8   G9

+340 ROME S.COSTANZA Φ   GOTHIC LOMBARDY AGL 12   LOMBARD TESTONA AGL·110   -570 NAUKRATIS JHS·1924·XI

G 26   G7

+580 THEUDELINDA GCK 12   +500? JAPAN RAR·1923 App Liii   +200?. NEUMAGEN EG 5149   +480 BABISKA BNS·1·178

G3   G4   G6

+451 MILAN,S.AQUILINO   +750 ROME WM·178   +600 NOCERA COMB M·A·1919,285

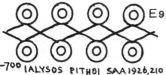

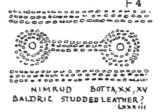

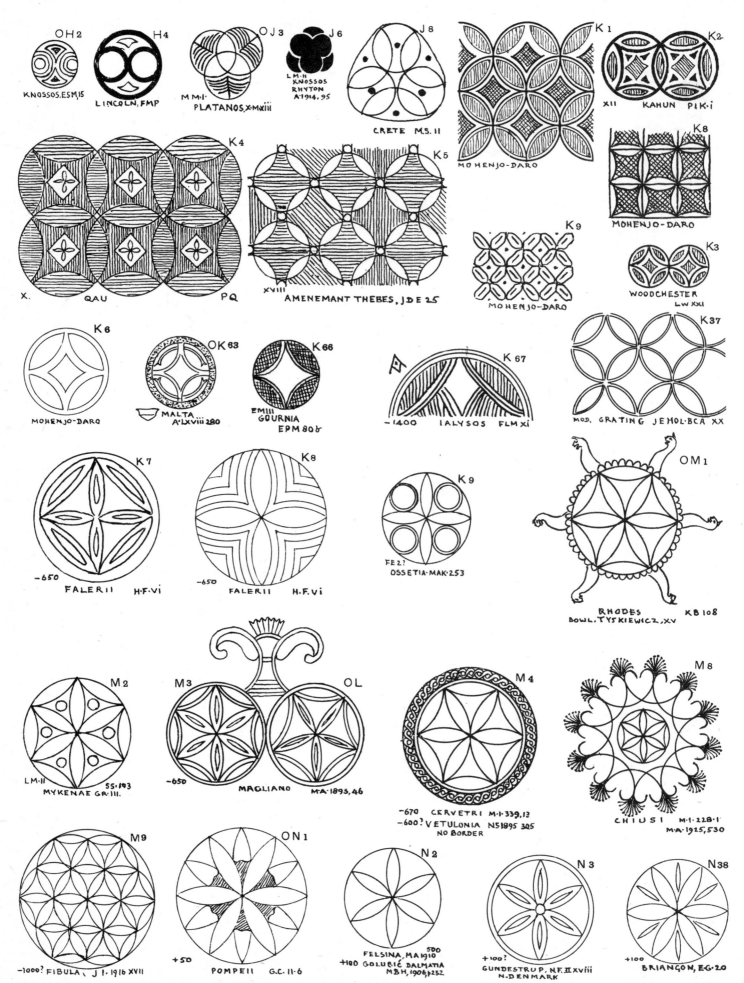

OH2   KNOSSOS.ESM.15

H4   LINCOLN, FMP

OJ3   MM.I   PLATANOS.X.MXIII

J6   LM.II KNOSSOS RHYTON A.1914.95

J8   CRETE M.S.11

K1   MOHENJO-DARO

K2   XII   KAHUN PIK.I

K4   X.   QAU   PQ

K5   XVIII   AMENEMANT THEBES, JDE 25

K8   MOHENJO-DARO

K9   MOHENJO-DARO

K3   WOODCHESTER LW XXI

K6   MOHENJO-DARO

OK63   MALTA A.LXVIII.280

K66   EMIII GOURNIA EPM 808

K67   -1400   IALYSOS FLM XI

K37   MOD. GRATING JEHOL BCA XX

K7   -650   FALERII   H.F.VI

K8   -650   FALERII   H.F.VI

K9   FE2?   OSSETIA.MAK.253

OM1   RHODES KB 108 BOWL.TYSKIEWICZ.XV

M2   LM.II 55.193   MYKENAE GR.III.

M3   -650   MAGLIANO M.A.1893,46   OL

M4   -670   CERVETRI M.I 339,13   -600? VETULONIA N51895 305 NO BORDER

M8   CHIUSI M.I 228.1 M.A.1925,530

M9   -1000? FIBULA, J1.1916 XVII

ON1   +50   POMPEII   G.C.11.6

N2   FELSINA, MA1910   500 +100 GOLUBIC DALMATIA MBH,1908,p232

N3   +100?   GUNDESTRUP, N.F.II XVIII N.DENMARK

N38   +100   BRIANCON, E.G.20

DURA C· XCI
+1400? ASCOLI CATHED.ʳ
COMMINGES E·G·879
+200? BONN E·G·6272
LOMBARD TOSCANA A·G·L·170
AQUILEIA NS,1927,276

+500? DABRAVINA MBH 1907,21
+850 AHENNY S·CROSS CCO·4A
NARCE·MA·1894,270
KHAZINEH C.ASIA MAK 968

P
SKIRLS

PP — EM I-II MOCHLOS S M 24
PQ1 — CRETE, MS III

Q3 — MM I X M XIV PLATANOS
Q5 — CRETE MS III

Q7 — MM I·PALAIKASTRO ABS,1923 SUPR XI
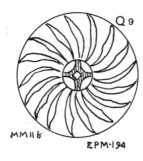
Q9 — MM II b EPM·194

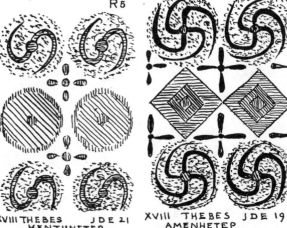
R5 / R6
XVIII THEBES MENTUHETEP JDE 21
XVIII THEBES AMENHETEP JDE 19

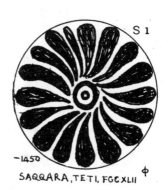
S1 — SAQQARA, TETI, FGCXLII
S2 — TROY S·1·1946
S3 — TROY S·1·1903
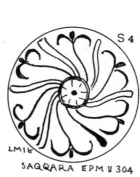
S4 — SAQQARA EPM II 304 LM I b

XVIII THEBES NEKHT-MIN JDE 35 R7

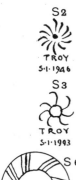
S6 — TROY, S·1·1837

S7 — LM I MYKENAE GR4, SS 226

S8 — LM I MYKENAE GR2·SS·207

S9 — LM I MYKENAE GR5·SS·257

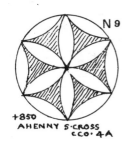

PT3

-1100
SYRACUSE
MA 1893 t1

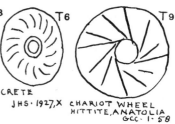

T6

CRETE
JHS·1927,X

T9

CHARIOT WHEEL
HITTITE, ANATOLIA
GCC·1·58

U1

-500 ANANINO
RV·I XXXVI

U3

-500
S·MAURO SICILY MA 1910.VI

U6

-650?
IALYSOS SAA 1926·187
BEFORE
+870 S·CLEMENTE, ROME FE 2? OSSETIA·MAK, CVIII
-200? KERTCH RK·XXIV

U9

-550?
IALYSOS
SAA 1926·192

V2

-700
CUMA
MA·1913 XLVII

V3

NARCE· MA 1894 288

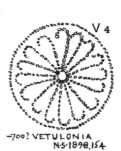

V4

-700? VETULONIA
N·S 1898,154

V5

FLORENCE, M·AA·I·XVII,2
GRANULAR WOR·

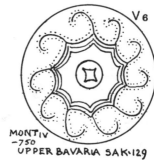

V6

MONT IV
-750
UPPER BAVARIA SAK·129

V7

-650
FALERII HF VI

V8

-1100,200 SCV 60
CHINA

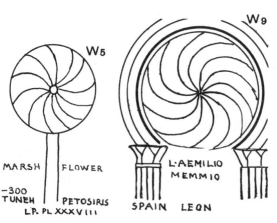

W2

-250 ORENBURG RI·G·XXIV
PERSIAN

W5

MARSH FLOWER

-300
TUNEH PETOSIRIS
LP. PL XXXVIII

W9

L·AEMILIO
MEMMIO
SPAIN LEON

X1

-130?
AYLESFORD
BMCE 93

X2

-100
SOMME
BMCE·þl III

X3

GOTHIC AFW·23
S.E. NORWAY

X5

+500 OXYRHYNKHOS PTC.XLV

X6

+500?
KAMMUNTA
CC·III·XXI

X7

NARBONNE
EG 6901,6908

X8

682 ROME
S·GIORG·VEL
SEE SY6 FP.

Y2

+650
OR
750 FP
ROME, S·MARIA ANT

Y4

+7--
MODENA
CATHEDRAL

Y6

+770
CIVIDALE S·MARIA ϕ

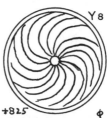

Y8

+825
ROME S·SABINA ϕ
+513 CLEMENTINUS
DIPTYCH·DCD XVI
+525 PHILOXENUS
DRESS.DCD,XXIX

Z1

+800? ATHENS
MAIA, 1906 VII

Z3

INISBOFINNE
CCO 9 F

Z5

CLONMACNOISE
CCO 9 G

Z7

RHEFERT CCO.9.1
GLENDALOCH

Z9

LOCHLEE SCOTLAND
MLW D·415

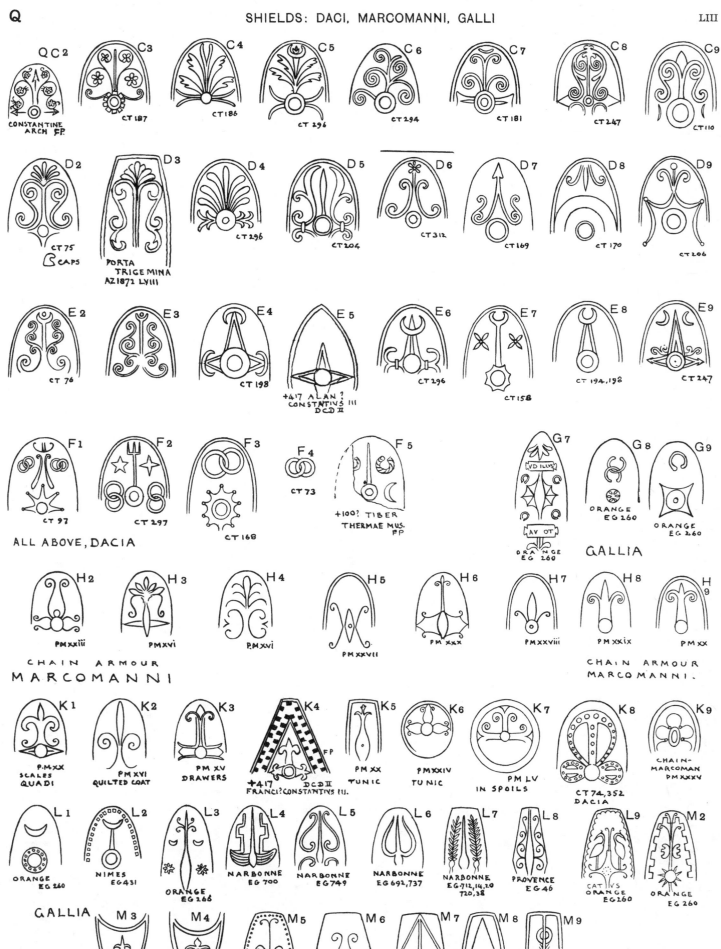

QP2

±⁰ THAMES
BMCE i

P4
CORNUFICIA
BRC i
JUNO SOSPITA
LANUVINA

P6
SHIELD
SENJERLI
~200
WAH XXIX

R2
+220? THERMAE
CARACALLA. F.R

R3

R4
PORTA
TRIGEMINA
AZ·1872 LVIII

R5
DACIA
CT 73

R6
CT

R7
CT 181

R8
CT 196

R9
CT 181

PORTA
TRIGEMINA
AZ·1872 LVIII

T2
CAECILIA, BRC 28,30
MACEDONIAN

T3
MACEDONIAN
ROMAN

T4
SPARTA ABS

T5
±⁰
ARLES EG 127

T6
CAESAR
JULIA BRC·164

V2
+50
SENS. EG 2761

V3
+50
SENS EG 2761

V4
−50?
MEAUX EG3207

V5
PORTA TRIGEMINA
AZ·1872 LVIII

V6
±⁰
PROVENCE, EG 46

V7
COMMINGES

V8
EG 843

FOR SCOTTISH
SHIELDS
SEE LXXXVII QZ

X1
+200? FIBULA KENCHESTER
JRS 1925 XXXIV

X2
BERLIN   S·T·V
SCYTHIAN AND DRAGON

X3
DACIA
CT 68

X4
TERMISOS
PISIDIA
JOAI·1900,184

X5
VAISON EG 295
BEZIERS 433

Y1
WOODCHESTER
LW·VII

+400
RUSGUNIAS
AJA 1920 152

Y14

X6
ETRUSCAN
PERUGIA
KUE II LXXXI

X7
ETRUSCAN
PERUGIA
KUE II LXXXIV

X8
+300
FIBULA
SOMERSET
JRS,1925,230

X9
TERMISSOS
PISIDIA
JOAI·1900,185

Y2
CAPRI M·A·1923,338

Y3
+150?
KÖNIGSHOFFEN   EG 5518

Y4
+40 SALZBURG
AJA 1920,152

Y5
+430 S·MATRONA CAPUA   Φ

Y6
THEODORIC, RAVENNA
M·A·1916,750

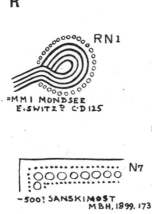

RN1
=MM I MONDSEE
E. SWITZ? C·D·125

N3
MM III
SITEIA EPM 371
SEE ME 2

N4
L·M·II
GR·III MYKENAE, S·S·149

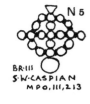

N5
BR·III
S·W·CASPIAN
MPO, III, 213

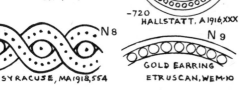

N6
-720
HALLSTATT, A 1916, XXX

N8
-600 SYRACUSE, MA1918,554

N9
GOLD EARRING
ETRUSCAN, WEM·10

N7
-500? SANSKIMOST
M B H, 1899, 173

RO2
-550
OLBIA, BEADS
JI·1914, 24b

O3
FE 2
BERGENHUS
R·A·N·668
SEE RQ3

O4
FE·2 BUSKERUD
R·A·N. 701

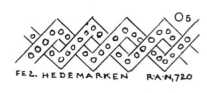

O5
FE 2. HEDEMARKEN   R·A·N, 720

P7

O6
WATSCH, CARNIOLA   B·C· 67

O7
-50 GLASTONBURY, BGG LXXiii

O8
-100? GLASTONBURY
POT   B.G.G. Lxxi

P1
+400?
GENEVA
LAMP. BAS II˟

P2
BAVARIA
AFW.242

P3
+400-700
SÖDERMANLAND
M·C·S· 129

P4
+414
KSEJBEH
B·N·S·I·170

P5
+525 DIPTYCH
PHILOXENUS
D·C·D·XXIX

P6
+462
DAR KITA   BN·S·I·196

+418 DAR KITA
B·N·S·I·189

Q1
MAINZ AFW, 275

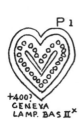

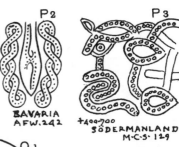

Q4

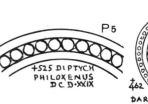

Q6
+600 TAPLOW   AAS·2

P84

P8
+650 BEHIOH SYRIA, CAI·23

P9
+600 NOCERA   A·1918, 210

+737
CIVIDALE ɸ

Q2
+650 FAVERSHAM
A·A·S· 250

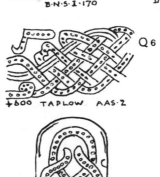

LOMBARD, BRESCIA
A·G·L, 2.74

Q5
+660
FRIESLAND
A·A·S· 291

Q7
+610
LANGENEHRINGEN, L·A·IV, 10

Q76

Q9
WURTEMBURG
A·F·W· 258

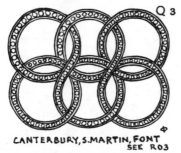

Q3
CANTERBURY, S. MARTIN, FONT
SEE RO3

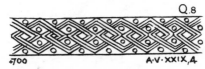

Q.8
-700   A·V·XXIX, 4

+630
RIJNSBURG, HOLLAND
A·A·S· 223

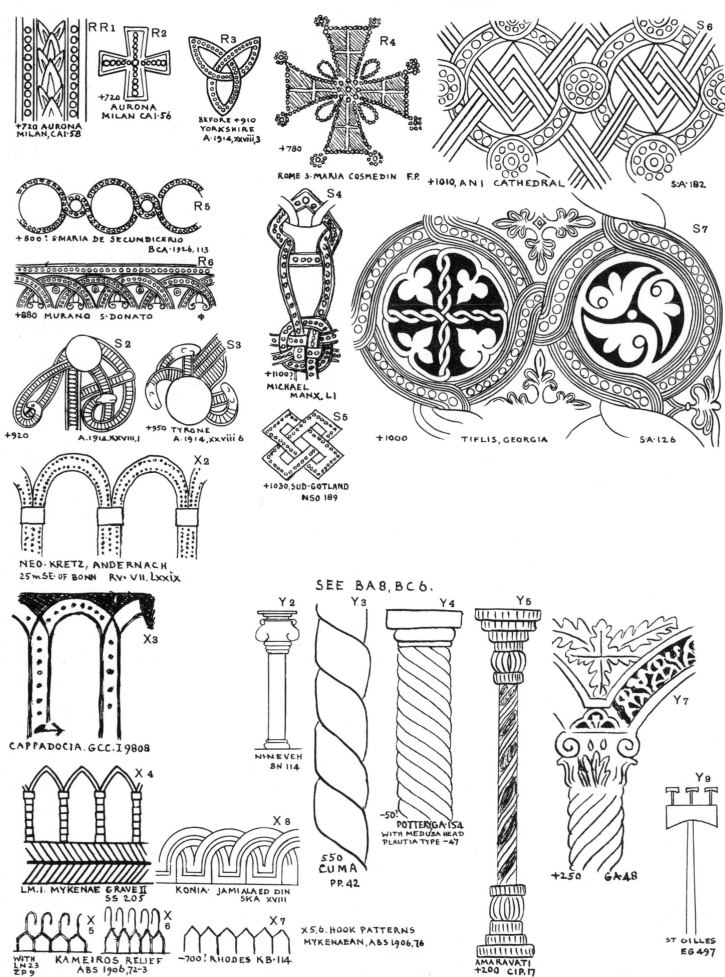

RR1   R2

+720 AURONA
MILAN, CA I. 58

AURONA
MILAN CA I. 56
+720

R3
BEFORE +910
YORKSHIRE
A.1914, xxviii 3

R4
+780
ROME S. MARIA COSMEDIN F.P.

S6
+1010, ANI CATHEDRAL   S.A.182

R5
+800? S. MARIA DE SECUNDICERIO
BCA.1926, 113

R6
+880 MURANO S. DONATO

S2
+920   A.1914, XXVIII, I

S3
+950 TYRONE
A.1914, xxviii 6

S4
+1100?
MICHAEL
MANX. LI

S5
+1030, SUD-GOTLAND
NSO 189

S7
+1000   TIFLIS, GEORGIA   S.A.126

X2
NEO. KRETZ, ANDERNACH
25 m SE. OF BONN   RV. VII. Lxxix

X3
CAPPADOCIA. GCC. I 9808

X4
LM.I. MYKENAE GRAVE II
SS 205

X8
KONIA. JAMIALAED DIN
SKA XVIII

X5   X6
WITH
LN23
ZP9   KAMEIROS RELIEF
ABS 1906, 72-3

X7
-700? RHODES KB.114

X5,6. HOOK PATTERNS
MYKENAEAN, ABS 1906, 76

SEE BA8, BC6.

Y2
NINEVEH
BN 114

Y3
550
CUMA
PP. 42

Y4
-50?
POTTERY GA. 154
WITH MEDUSA HEAD
PLAUTIA TYPE -47

Y5
AMARAVATI
+200 CIP. 17

Y7
+250   GA 48

Y9
ST GILLES
EG 497

SA1 SUSA DCL·XVI,3
A2 ARCHAIC, SUSA, DCL·XVi,12
A3 SUSA, DCL·XVi,9
A36 -3000 SUSA, MA·K·1318
A4 MOHEN·JO
A5 SUSA, DCL·XiV,5
A6 VIII PBS·275
A7 VIII PBS, 272

A8 CILICIA, PBS,iv
A9 ALEPPO, PBS iv
B2 MMI XMviii PORTI
B3 VIII PBS 221 EGYPT
B4 XIV PBS 152 EGYPT
B5 XV? PBS 255 B EGYPT
B6 VI RMA,XL AMRAH
B7 TSANI, WT·93
B8 LATIUM M·I·141,17

C1 EMi MOCHLOS. SM·6.
C2 EMi. S·M·9 MOCHLOS
C3 FMIII T·A·P·J·III·xxviii
C4 AL UBAID HWU·XVI
C5 MMI PLATANOS, XMXiii
C9 TROY S·I·1856
D1 MMI PLATANOS X·M· XIV
D2 MMI· KAMARES MGP. Lxi
C6 MMi· KUMASA XM·iv
C7 VIII EGYPT P·BS·220
C8 LENTOID ZERELIA MELOS WT.112

D3 MMI PLATANOS XM XIV
D4 CRETE M·S·XII
D5 MMi· KAMARES MGP. Lxii
D6 MM II EPM·194
D7 MMIII ABS X·2
D8 MM IIa EPM 194 KNOSSOS
D9 MMIIA EPM, 194

E2 MMi KUMASA X·M·Vi
E3 MM II C·D·93 AUNJETITZ SAXONY
E32 IRELAND JSH·160
E4 MMIII SITEIA EPM·371
E6 MYKENAE DCP 288
E8 LM·II· GR·III·MYKENAI B·A·K·312

F3 NEO· LAIBACH HB K·Vii
F4 MMIII KNOSSOS EPM·376
F5 MMIII EPM 374
F6 MMIII EPM 375
F7 MMIII KNOSSOS, MS47, EPM·II·456 ROBE
F8 MYKENAE. J·I·1919 ix ROBE

HAGHIA TRIADA   M·A·1903 X

XVIII AMENEMHAT EGYPT   JDE42

SH2

ABS.
PHYLAKOPI, xiii

MM CRETE K·M·

H6

MYKENAE
VASE
DCP 288

H8

-600?
PRAESOS
ABS·1906·41

H4

SJ1

MYKENAE
F.L.M XXVIII

J2

MYKENAE
F.L.M. XXVIII

J3

MYKENAE
F.L.M.XXVIII

J5

1500 GERAR
P.G.LXIV

J6

-1150?
CRETE MYKENAEAN COFFER
M·A·1889 I, 230

J8

1150? CRETE, M·A·1889, 230

J9

LM IIIa. TDAii
KNOSSOS

SK2

-800? N FOKORU HUNGARY   H.U.II 100

K4

-800?
FOKORU
CDP.385

K5 K6   ASSYRIA N   K8 K9   H.W.p.394

L1

BR.
CORNETO N
M·I· 276·16

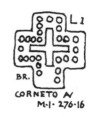

L2

VULCI, M·I·261

L25

-600?THARROS
BMJ

L4

ASSYRIA P.N.XXVIII
KHORSABAD

L35

-570 FIKELLURA DAFNE, P.D.XXVII

L3

-650
FALERII, HF·VI

L5

TENE III
SARAGOSSA
DF2·686

L6

-600
DAFNEH
P.D.XXV

L7

Fe·1
SILESIA
DF 333

L8

PALESTRINA, M·I·365·5

M1

-250
FICORONIAN CISTA, TOP. FP

M2

STAROBELSK
SCYTHIAN, R+G,20

M3

-600?
LADENBURG, BADEN
L·A·V, pl·48

M4

BOHEMIA. A.F.W. 34
IIIII GARNET

M5

+100?
CAERWENT
A·1902; X

M6

+200. NYDAM. EDE.N·ix

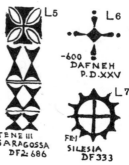

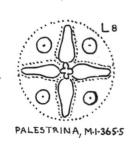

M7

250
ORENBURG
R·I·G·XXIV
(PERSIAN)

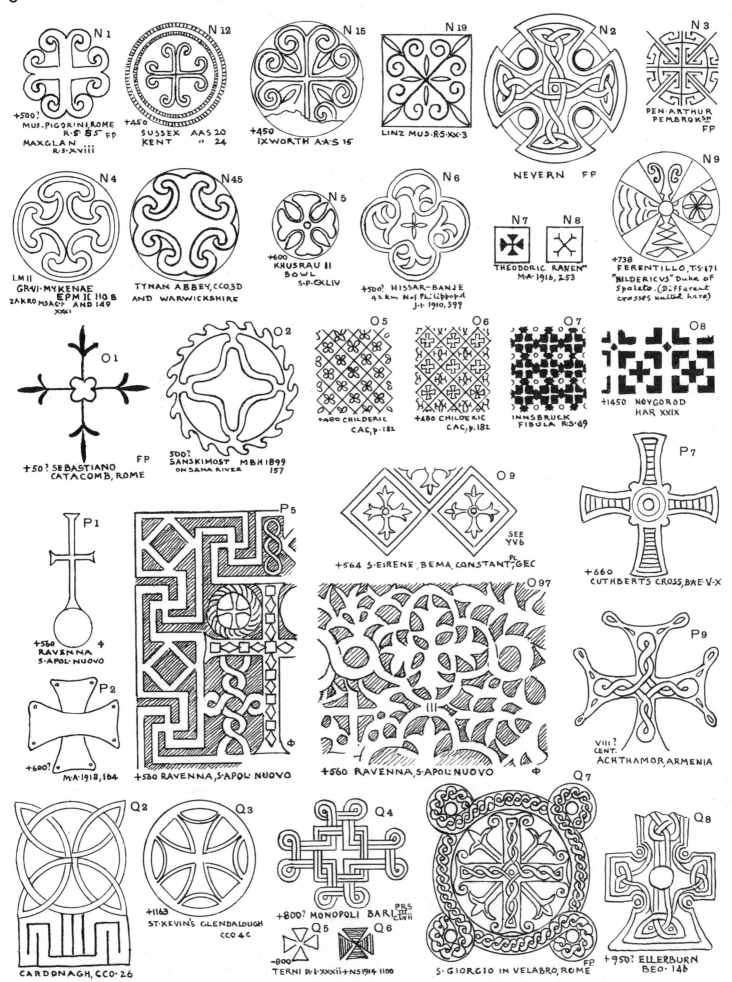

N 1
+500?
MUS. PIGORINI, ROME
R·S·85 FP
MAXGLAN
R·S·XVIII

N 12
+450
SUSSEX A·A·S 20
KENT   " 24

N 15
+450
IXWORTH A·A·S 15

N 19
LINZ MUS·R·S·XX·3

N 2
NEVERN   FP

N 3
PEN·ARTHUR
PEMBROKSH
FP

N 4
LM II
GR·VI·MYKENAE
EPM II 110 B
ZAKRO MSAG·T AND 149
XXXI

N 45
TYNAN ABBEY, CCO·3D
AND WARWICKSHIRE

N 5
+600
KHUSRAU II
BOWL
S·P·CXLIV

N 6
+500? HISSAR-BANJE
42 km N of Philibbopol
J·I·1910,399

N 7   N 8
THEODORIC RAVEN
M·A·1916,253

N 9
+738
FERENTILLO, T·S·171
"HILDERICVS" Duke of
Spoleto. (Different
crosses united here)

O 1
+50? SEBASTIANO   FP
CATACOMB, ROME

O 2
500?
SANSKIMOST MBH 1899
ON SAMA RIVER   157

O 5
+480 CHILDERIC
CAC, p·182

O 6
+480 CHILDERIC
CAC, p·182

O 7
INNSBRUCK
FIBULA R·S·69

O 8
+1450 NOVGOROD
HAR XXIX

O 9
+564 S·EIRENE, BEMA, CONSTANT, GEC
SEE YVb

P 7
+660
CUTHBERTS CROSS, BAE·V·X

P 1
+560
RAVENNA
S·APOL·NUOVO

P 5
+560 RAVENNA, S·APOL·NUOVO

P 2
+600?
M·A·1918,164

O 97
+560 RAVENNA, S·APOL·NUOVO

P 9
VIII?
CENT.
ACHTHAMOR, ARMENIA

Q 2
CARDONAGH, CCO·26

Q 3
+1163
ST·KEVIN'S GLENDALOUGH
CCO 4 C

Q 4
+800? MONOPOLI BARI

Q 5   Q 6
~800
TERNI R·I·xxxii + NS 1914 1100

Q 7
S·GIORGIO IN VELABRO, ROME   FP

Q 8
+950? ELLERBURN
BEO·14b

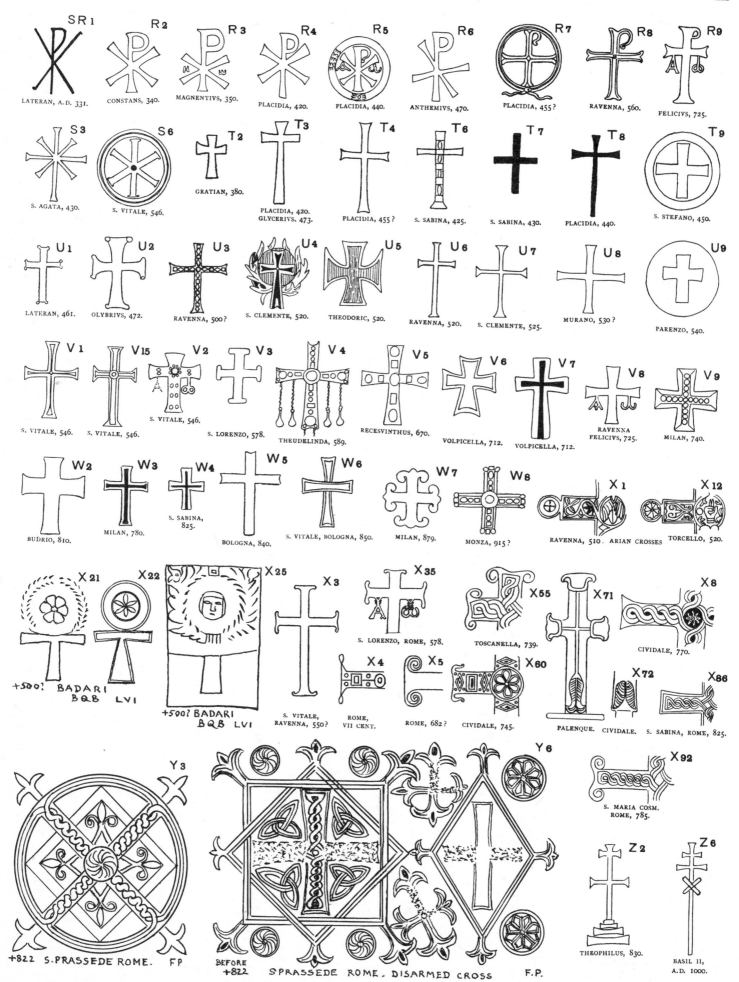

SR1 — LATERAN, A.D. 331.
R2 — CONSTANS, 340.
R3 — MAGNENTIVS, 350.
R4 — PLACIDIA, 420.
R5 — PLACIDIA, 440.
R6 — ANTHEMIVS, 470.
R7 — PLACIDIA, 455?
R8 — RAVENNA, 560.
R9 — FELICIVS, 725.

S3 — S. AGATA, 430.
S6 — S. VITALE, 546.
T2 — GRATIAN, 380.
T3 — PLACIDIA, 420. GLYCERIVS, 473.
T4 — PLACIDIA, 455?
T6 — S. SABINA, 425.
T7 — S. SABINA, 430.
T8 — PLACIDIA, 440.
T9 — S. STEFANO, 450.

U1 — LATERAN, 461.
U2 — OLYBRIVS, 472.
U3 — RAVENNA, 500?
U4 — S. CLEMENTE, 520.
U5 — THEODORIC, 520.
U6 — RAVENNA, 520.
U7 — S. CLEMENTE, 525.
U8 — MURANO, 530?
U9 — PARENZO, 540.

V1 — S. VITALE, 546.
V15 — S. VITALE, 546.
V2 — S. VITALE, 546.
V3 — S. LORENZO, 578.
V4 — THEUDELINDA, 589.
V5 — RECESVINTHUS, 670.
V6 — VOLPICELLA, 712.
V7 — VOLPICELLA, 712.
V8 — RAVENNA FELICIVS, 725.
V9 — MILAN, 740.

W2 — BUDRIO, 810.
W3 — MILAN, 780.
W4 — S. SABINA, 825.
W5 — BOLOGNA, 840.
W6 — S. VITALE, BOLOGNA, 850.
W7 — MILAN, 879.
W8 — MONZA, 915?
X1 — RAVENNA, 510. ARIAN CROSSES
X12 — TORCELLO, 520.

X21 — +500? BADARI BQB LVI
X22 — BADARI BQB LVI
X25 — +500? BADARI BQB LVI
X3 — S. VITALE, RAVENNA, 550?
X35 — S. LORENZO, ROME, 578.
X55 — TOSCANELLA, 739.
X71
X8 — CIVIDALE, 770.
X4 — ROME, VII CENT.
X5 — ROME, 682?
X60 — CIVIDALE, 745.
X72 — PALENQUE. CIVIDALE.
X86 — S. SABINA, ROME, 825.

Y3 — +822 S. PRASSEDE ROME. FP
Y6 — BEFORE +822 S PRASSEDE ROME. DISARMED CROSS F.P.
X92 — S. MARIA COSM. ROME, 785.
Z2 — THEOPHILUS, 830.
Z6 — BASIL II, A.D. 1000.

TA1 AL UBAID HWUXVII

A2 EM II MOCHLOS EPM.42

A3 VI ABYDOS PBS 226

A3 EM II-III MOCHLOS S·M·13

A36 CAPPADOCIA GCC II.210,10206 SEE YO

A4 1600? CYPRUS, K·B·80

A5 M.M.I. PLATANOS. X·M·X

A6 -1200? BRITAIN A·B·A·xxiv 57

A9 FALERII M·I·326,2

A7 ALMIZARAQUE S·O·O·V.

A76 -900? BRITAIN A·B·A·xxiii, 24

A88 JEMDET NASR -3000

A96 BR. CHAUCHITZA A·1925,xxviii MACEDONIA

A8 -2000? ARENA CANDIDE M·I·110·21 -750 GERAR P·G·XL TIRYNS SCHLIEM. XVI

A86 -900 BISENZIO M·I·256

F2 AL UBAID HW·U·XVIII

F3 ARCHAIC SUSA DCL·XV·4

F4 -3000? NAL BALUCHI EM

F6 CONSTANTINOVO, SCYTHIC, M·S·G·25

F7 ARCHAIC SUSA DCL·XV·5

F8 TEPE MUSSIAN MAK 896

F9 GCC I·14 CAPPADOCIA GCC·17

G1 DIPYLON -800? ATHENS

G2 -750 GERAR P·G·XLI

G3 +600 NOCERA, M·A·1918, 210

G4 +600 NOCERA, M·A·1918·210

G5 S· OF PO M·I·24·12

G6 -700? RHODES K·B·115

G7 -600 MT SAN NACE, APULIA GBA·VI.6

G8 FE2 BERGEN HUS R·A·N·740

G9 GOTHIC PICENO. A·G·L·5

H1 CHAERONEA WT.140

H11 STEPAN-ZMINDA GCC I·LV GEORGIA CA F·28

H18 FE·I· SILESIA, DF. 333

H15 -3000? DAMGHAN TEHERAN I·L·N·1929, V, 25

H2 EM III CYCLAD. SYROS C·D·20

H3 MORBIHAN M·B·H·1912·27

H4 FE·I· OEDENBURG HUNGARY HBK xxiii

H7 -700? IALYSOS, SAA 1926 PITHOI 209

H8 AMORGOS K·B·83

H5 EB IRELAND LUNULA AGO·I

H52 -1200 BRITAIN A·B·A·xxiii 9

H56 -750 GERAR P·G·XLI MÜGLITZ

H6 -570 NAUKRATIS JHS 1924 XI

H87 -900? BRITAIN A·B·A·CV·109

H9 -900? BRITAIN A·B·A·CV·67

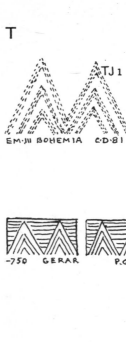

TJ1

EM·III BOHEMIA C·D·81

J2

CAPPADOCIA G·C·I·11

J3

S·OF PO   M·I·24·13

J4

DAUNIA M·AP·XiV·2
LATIUM M·I·140·9

J25

MOHENJO-DARO

J6

-750 GERAR   P.G. xLi

J7

FE.I. LANGELEBARN
LOWER AUSTRIA
CA 20

J8

-800   CUMA   M·A·1913,Xi

J9

-750 GERAR   P.G. xLi

K2

VOLTERRA. M·I·171·2

K3

-1200-600 ?
BRITAIN
A.B.A.XXIII 2,51
122180

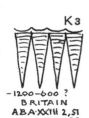

K5

-1200? BRITAIN
A·B·A XXV, 121

K7

-1200? BRITAIN
A·B·A·XXIII. 12

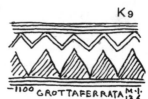

K8

PORTUGAL S·OO·Vi

K9

-1100 GROTTAFERRATA M·I·
136

L1

-600?   M·G·

L2

-800?   M·G

L3

FALERII   M·A·1894·187

L4

-700? BRITAIN
A·B·A,CVI,1b9

L5

QUERCIANELLA   M·I·169·19

L6

MID APULIA
M·AP·XX·7

L8

LMIII LIANOKLADHI
WT 32

L9

QUERCIANELLA   M·I·169·19

N1

LATIUM CORNETO
M·I·141 M·I·277

N2

-1100,200 CHINA SCV 68

N3

MID APULIA.   M·AP·XX·14

N4 N5

-570 NAUKRATIS
JHS'1924·Xi

N6

-600
P·NK·V

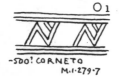

N7

600 SYRACUSE
-M·A·1918,536

N8

MID APULIA   M·AP·XX·3

N9

GALLEN PRIORY
C·C·O·7c

O1

-500! CORNETO
M·I·279·7

O2

+890 CLONMACNOISE
B·A·E·V·5

O3

+890 CLONMACNOISE
B·A·E·V·5

O4

+950 CLONMACNOISE
B·A·E·V·5

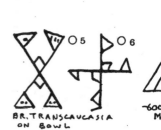

O5 O6

BR. TRANSCAUCASIA
ON BOWL
Z·E·1905 142

O7

-3500 UR

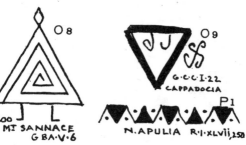

O8

-600
MT SANNACE
G·BA·V·6

O9

G·C·C·I·22
CAPPADOCIA

P1

N. APULIA R·I·XLVii,25a

P2

-500 CORNETO, M·I·279 7

P3

N. APULIAN. M·AP·XVii 10

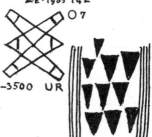

P4

CAPPADOCIA
G·C·C·I·74

P5

CAPPADOCIA
G·C·C·II 9451

P6

CAPPADOCIA G·C·I·73

P8

FE I
OEDENBURG
HUNGARY
D·F·218

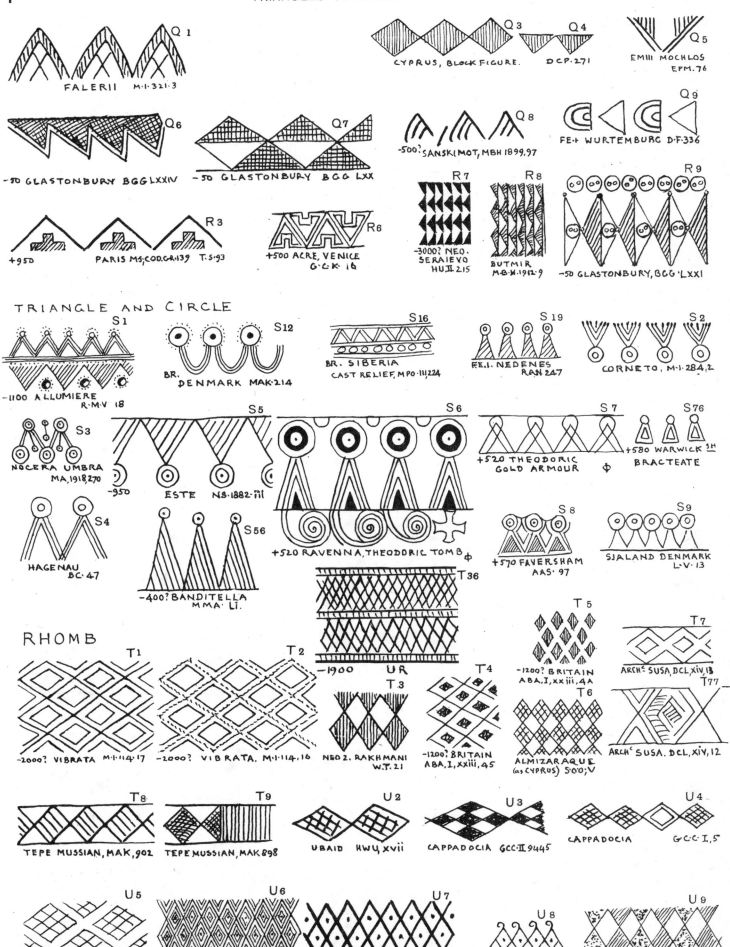

Q 1
FALERII   M·I·321·3

Q 3
Q 4
CYPRUS, BLOCK FIGURE.   DCP·271

Q 5
EM III MOCHLOS
EPM·76

Q 6
-50 GLASTONBURY BGG LXXIV

Q 7
-50 GLASTONBURY BGG LXX

Q 8
-500? SANSKI MOT, MBH 1899,97

Q 9
FE·I WURTEMBURG D·F·336

R 3
+950   PARIS MS; COD.GR·139   T.S·93

R 6
+500 ACRE, VENICE
G·C·K·16

R 7
-3000? NEO.
SERAIEVO
HU·II·215

R 8
BUTMIR
M.B.H.1912·9

R 9
-50 GLASTONBURY, BGG·LXXI

TRIANGLE AND CIRCLE

S 1
-1100 ALLUMIERE
R.M.V·18

S 12
BR.
DENMARK MAK·214

S 16
BR. SIBERIA
CAST RELIEF, MPO·III,224

S 19
FE.I. NEDENES
RAN 247

S 2
CORNETO, M·I·284,2

S 3
NOCERA UMBRA
MA, 1918,270

S 5
-950   ESTE   NS·1882-711

S 6
+520 RAVENNA, THEODORIC TOMB Φ

S 7
+520 THEODORIC
GOLD ARMOUR   Φ

S 76
+580 WARWICK SH
BRACTEATE

S 4
HAGENAU
BC·47

S 56
-400? BANDITELLA
MMA Li.

S 8
+570 FAVERSHAM
AAS·97

S 9
SJALAND DENMARK
L·V·13

T 36
-1900   UR

RHOMB

T 1
-2000? VIBRATA M·I·114·17

T 2
-2000? VIBRATA, M·I·114,16

T 3
NEO 2. RAKHMANI
W.T. 21

T 4
-1200? BRITAIN
ABA,I, xxiii, 45

T 5
-1200? BRITAIN
ABA,I, xxiii,4A

T 6
ALMIZARAQUE
(as CYPRUS) S·O·O; V

T 7
ARCH^c SUSA, DCL, xiv,13

T 77
ARCH^c SUSA, DCL, xiv, 12

T 8
TEPE MUSSIAN, MAK,902

T 9
TEPE MUSSIAN, MAK 898

U 2
UBAID   HWU xvii

U 3
CAPPADOCIA GCC·II 9445

U 4
CAPPADOCIA
G·C·C·I,5

U 5
-1200? BRITAIN
ABA,I, xxiv,60

U 6
-700   CRETE ABS viii

U 7
FALERII M·I·320, 14

U 8
-700 ATHENS K·B·116

U 9
CAPUA   K.T. 50

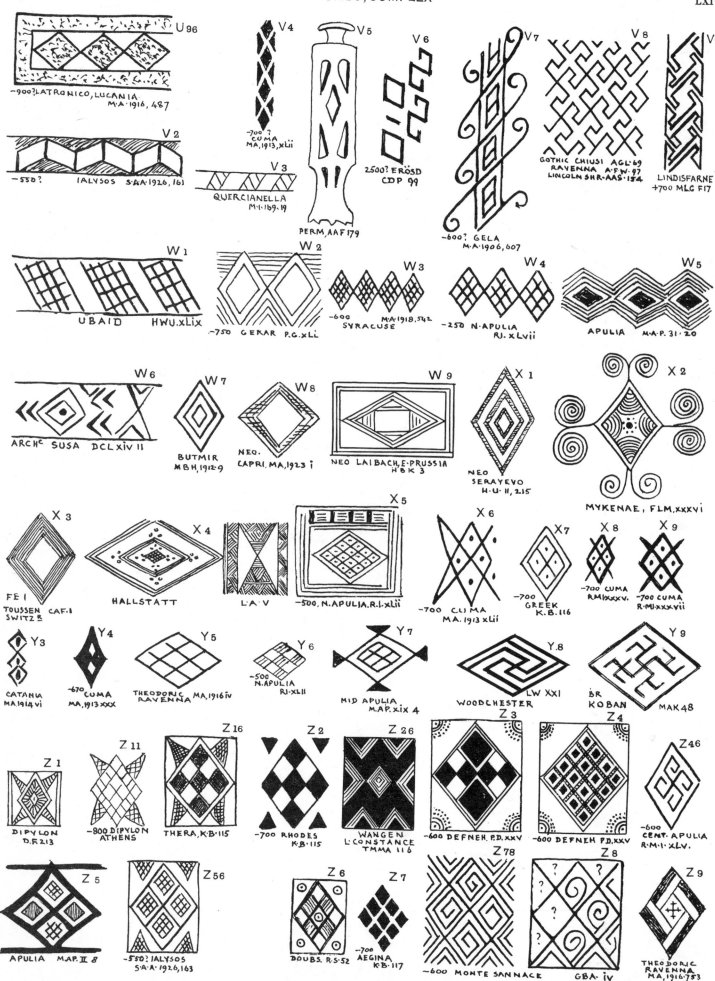

U 96   -900? LATRONICO, LUCANIA M·A·1916, 487

V 2   -550?   IALYSOS   S·A·A·1926, 161

V 3   QUERCIANELLA M·I·169·19

V 4   -700? CUMA MA, 1913, xLii

V 5   PERM, AAF 179

V 6   2500? ERÖSD CDP 99

V 7   -600? GELA M·A·1906, 607

V 8   GOTHIC CHIUSI AGL· 69 RAVENNA A·FW· 97 LINCOLN SHR·AAS·154

V 9   LINDISFARNE +700 MLG F17

W 1   UBAID   HWU· xLix

W 2   -750 GERAR P·G· xLi

W 3   -600   M·A·1918, 542 SYRACUSE

W 4   -250 N·APULIA RJ· x Lvii

W 5   APULIA   M·A·P. 31· 20

W 6   ARCH^c SUSA   DCL XiV II

W 7   BUTMIR MBH, 1912·9

W 8   NEO. CAPRI, MA, 1923 i

W 9   NEO LAIBACH, E·PRUSSIA HBK 3

X 1   NEO SERAYEVO H·U· II, 215

X 2   MYKENAE, FLM, xxxvi

X 3   FE I TOUSSEN CAF·I SWITZ^R

X 4   HALLSTATT

  L·A·V

X 5   -500, N.APULIA R.I· x Lii

X 6   -700 CUMA MA. 1913 x Lii

X 7   -700 GREEK K·B· 116

X 8   -700 CUMA RM lxxxv·

X 9   -700 CUMA R·M· xxxvii

Y 3   CATANIA MA·1914 vi

Y 4   -670 CUMA MA, 1913 xxx

Y 5   THEODORIC MA, 1916 iv RAVENNA

Y 6   -500 N·APULIA RJ· xLii

Y 7   MID APULIA M·AP· xix 4

Y 8   WOODCHESTER LW XXI

Y 9   BR KOBAN   MAK 48

Z 1   DIPYLON D·F· 213

Z 11   -800 DIPYLON ATHENS

Z 16   THERA, K·B· 115

Z 2   -700 RHODES K·B· 115

Z 26   WANGEN L·CONSTANCE TMMA 116

Z 3   -600 DEFNEH P·D· xxv

Z 4   -600 DEFNEH P·D· xxv

Z 46   -600 CENT. APULIA R·M·I· xLV.

Z 5   APULIA   M·AP· II 8

Z 56   -550? IALYSOS S·A·A·1926, 163

Z 6   DOUBS. R·S· 52

Z 7   -700 AEGINA K·B· 117

Z 78   -600 MONTE SAN NACE

Z 8   GBA· iv

Z 9   THEODORIC RAVENNA MA, 1916·753

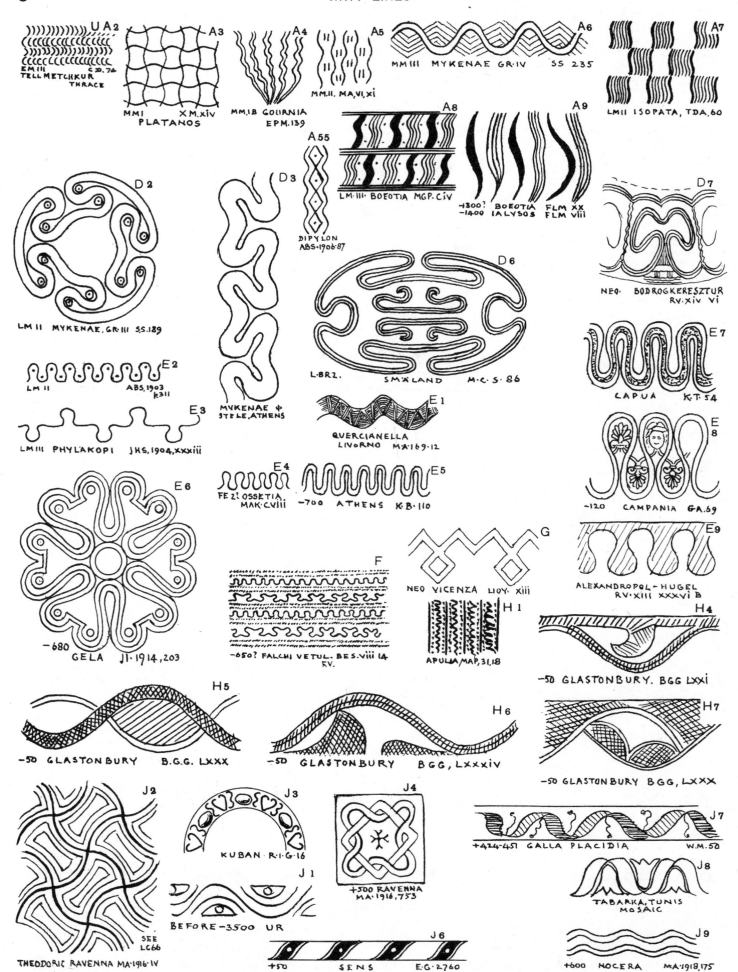

UA2
EM.III
TELL METCHKUR
THRACE   C 20.74

A3
MM.I   XM.xiv
PLATANOS

A4
MM.IB GOURNIA
EPM.139

A5
MM.II. MA.VI.xi

A6
MM.III MYKENAE GR.IV   SS 235

A7
LM.II ISOPATA, TDA.60

A8
LM.III. BOEOTIA MGP.CIV

A9
+1300? BOEOTIA FLM XX
−1400 IALYSOS FLM viii

A.55
DIPYLON
ABS.1906.87

D2
LM II MYKENAE, GR.III S.S.189

D3
MYKENAE φ
STELE, ATHENS

D6
L.BR2.   SMÄLAND   M.C.S.86

D7
NEO. BODROGKERESZTUR
RV.xiv vi

E2
LM II   ABS,1903
k.311

E3
LM III PHYLAKOPI   JHS,1904,xxxiii

E7
CAPUA   K.T.54

E8
CAMPANIA   GA.69
−120

E6
−680
GELA   J1.1914,203

E4
FE 2? OSSETIA.
MAK.CVIII

E5
−700 ATHENS K.B.110

E1
QUERCIANELLA
LIVORNO MA.169.12

E9
ALEXANDROPOL−HUGEL
RV.XIII XXXVI B

F
−050? FALCHI VETUL. BES.viii 14
F.V.

G
NEO VICENZA LIOY. xiii

H1
APULIA,MAP,31,18

H4
−50 GLASTONBURY. BGG LXXI

H5
−50 GLASTONBURY   B.G.G. LXXX

H6
−50 GLASTONBURY   BGG, LXXXIV

H7
−50 GLASTONBURY BGG, LXXX

J2
THEODORIC RAVENNA MA.1916. IV   SEE LC66

J3
KUBAN R.I.G.16

J4
+500 RAVENNA
MA.1916,753

J1
BEFORE −3500 UR

J6
+50   SENS   E.G.2760

J7
+424−451 GALLA PLACIDIA   W.M.50

J8
TABARKA,TUNIS
MOSAIC

J9
+600 NOCERA   MA.1918,175

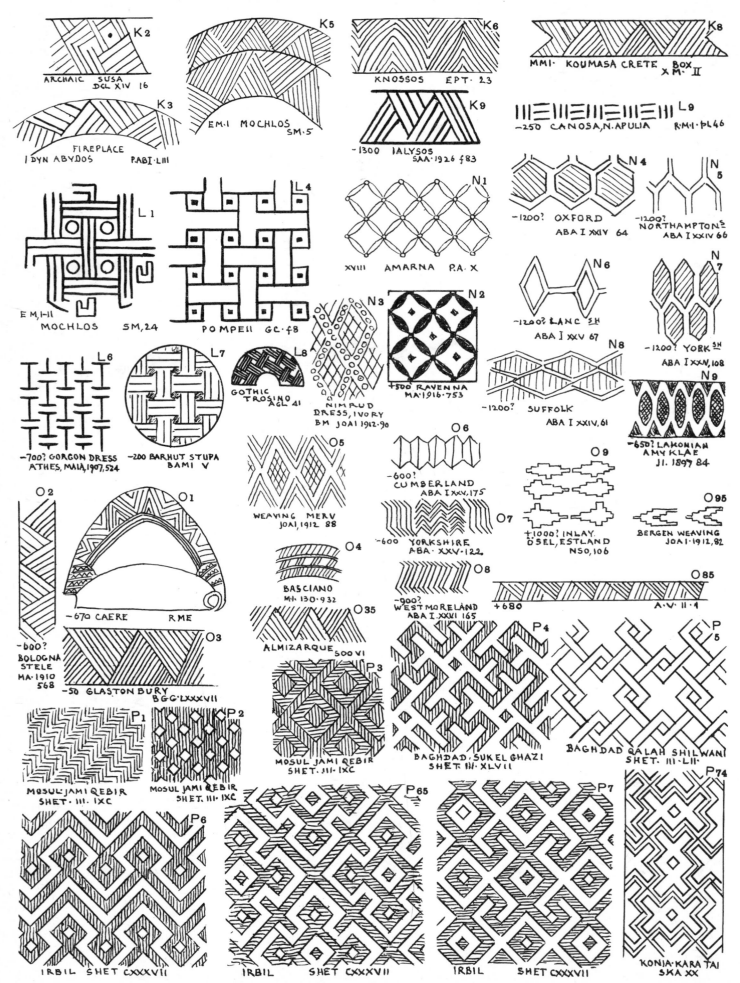

K2 — ARCHAIC SUSA DCL XIV 16

K3 — FIREPLACE I DYN ABYDOS P.ABI·LIII

K5 — EM·I MOCHLOS SM·5

K6 — KNOSSOS EPT·23

K9 — -1300 IALYSOS SAA·1926 f83

K8 — MMI· KOUMASA CRETE BOX X M·II

L9 — -250 CANOSA, N. APULIA R·M·I·PL46

L1 — EM,I-II MOCHLOS SM,24

L4 — POMPEII GC·f8

N1 — XVIII AMARNA P.A. X

N4 — -1200? OXFORD ABA I XXIV 64

N5 — -1200? NORTHAMPTONᵉ ABA I XXIV 66

N6 — -1200? LANC SH ABA I XXV 67

N7 — -1200? YORK SH ABA I XXIV, 108

L6 — -700? GORGON DRESS ATHES, MAIA,1907,524

L7 — -200 BARHUT STUPA BAMI V

L8 — GOTHIC TROSINO AGL 41

N3 — NIMRUD DRESS, IVORY BM JOAI 1912·90

N2 — +500 RAVENNA MA·1916·753

N8 — -1200? SUFFOLK ABA I XXIV, 61

N9 — -650? LAKONIAN AMYKLAE JI. 1897 84

O5 — WEAVING MERV JOAI, 1912 88

O6 — -600? CUMBERLAND ABA I XXV,175

O7 — -600 YORKSHIRE ABA· XXV·122

O9 — +1000? INLAY. ÖSEL, ESTLAND NSO,106

O95 — BERGEN WEAVING JOAI·1912,82

O2

O1 — -670 CAERE R ME

O3 — -50 GLASTONBURY B.G.G·LXXXVII

O4 — BASCIANO M·I·130·932

O8 — -900? WESTMORELAND ABA I·XXVI 165

O85 — +680 A·V·II·1

O35 — ALMIZARQUE 500 VI

-600? BOLOGNA STELE MA·1910 568

P4 — BAGHDAD, SUKEL GHAZI SHET III· XLVII

P5 — BAGHDAD QALAH SHILWANI SHET· III·LII·

P3 — MOSUL JAMI QEBIR SHET·III·IXC

P1 — MOSUL JAMI QEBIR SHET·III· IXC

P2 — MOSUL JAMI QEBIR SHET·III· IXC

P6 — IRBIL SHET CXXXVII

P65 — IRBIL SHET CXXXVII

P7 — IRBIL SHET CXXXVII

P74 — KONIA·KARA TAI SKA XX

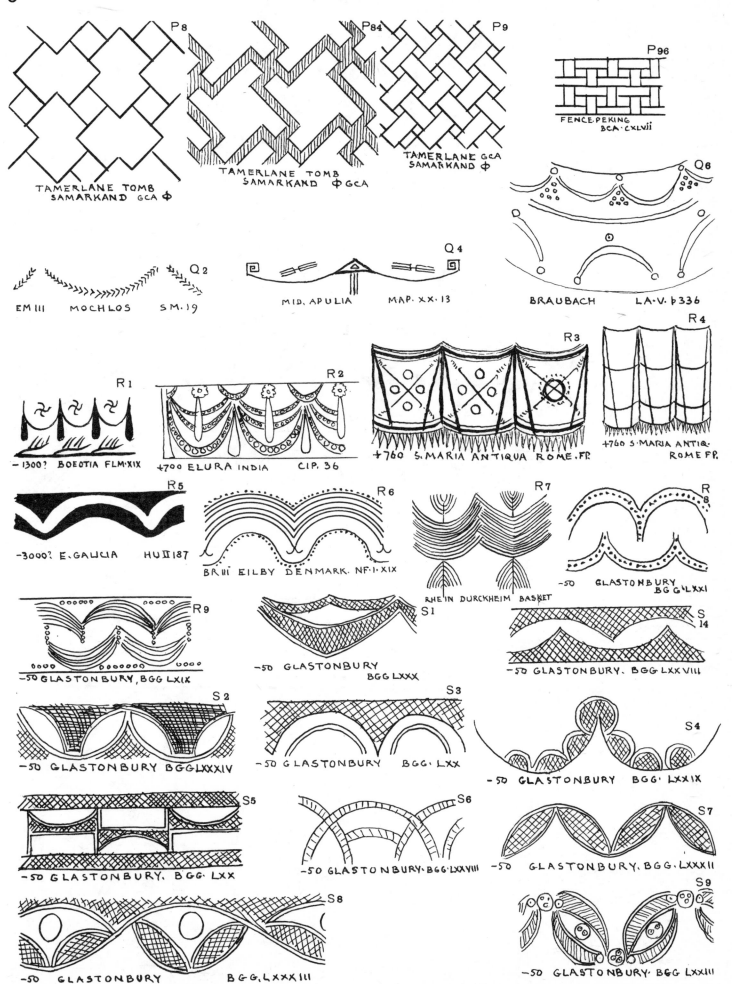

P8   P84   P9

P96

FENCE·PEKING BCA·CXLVii

TAMERLANE TOMB SAMARKAND GCA Φ

TAMERLANE TOMB SAMARKAND ΦGCA

TAMERLANE GCA SAMARKAND Φ

Q6

Q2

EM III   MOCHLOS   SM.19

Q4

MID. APULIA   MAP. XX·13

BRAUBACH   LA·V· þ336

R1

-1300? BOEOTIA FLM·XIX

R2

+700 ELURA INDIA   CIP. 36

R3

+760 S. MARIA ANTIQUA ROME.FR.

R4

+760 S. MARIA ANTIQ. ROME FP.

R5

-3000? E. GALICIA   HUII187

R6

BRIII EILBY DENMARK. NF·I·XIX

R7

RHEIN DURCKHEIM BASKET

R8

-50 GLASTONBURY BGG·LXXI

R9

-50 GLASTONBURY, BGG LXIX

S1

-50 GLASTONBURY BGG LXXX

S14

-50 GLASTONBURY. BGG LXXVIII

S2

-50 GLASTONBURY BGGLXXXIV

S3

-50 GLASTONBURY   BGG. LXX

S4

-50 GLASTONBURY   BGG. LXXIX

S5

-50 GLASTONBURY. BGG. LXX

S6

-50 GLASTONBURY. BGG LXXVIII

S7

-50 GLASTONBURY. BGG. LXXXII

S8

-50 GLASTONBURY   BGG. LXXXIII

S9

-50 GLASTONBURY· BGG LXXIII

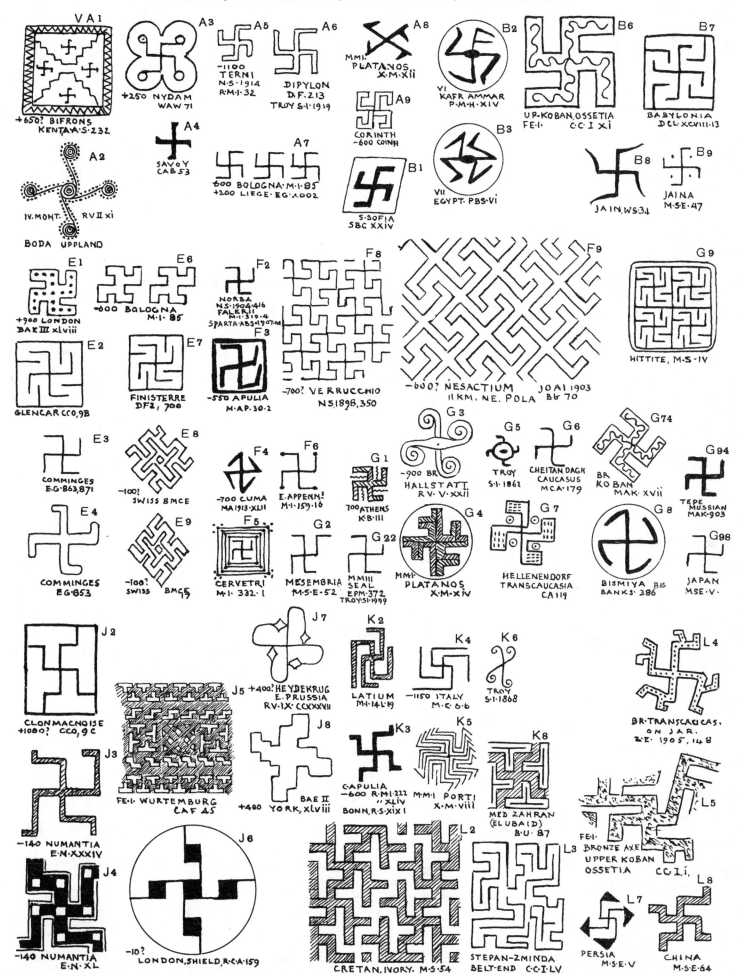

VA1
+650? BIFRONS
KENTAA S·232

A2
IV. MONT. RVIIxi
BODA UPPLAND

A3
+250 NYDAM
WAW 71

A4
SAVOY
CAB 53

A5
-1100
TERNI
N·S·1914
R·M·1·32

A6
DIPYLON
D.F.213
TROY S·I·1919

A7
-600 BOLOGNA·M·I·85
+200 LIEGE·EG·1002

A8
MM1·
PLATANOS
X·M·XII

A9
CORINTH
-600 COIN H

B1
S·SOFIA
SBC XXIV

B2
VI
KAFR AMMAR
P·M·H·XIV

B3
VII
EGYPT·PBS·VI

B6
UP-KOBAN, OSSETIA
FE·I·   C·C·I·Xi

B7
BABYLONIA
D·C·L·XCVIII·13

B8
JAIN,WS·34

B9
JAINA
M·S·E·47

E1
+900 LONDON
BAK III xlviii

E2
GLENCAR CCO,9B

E3
COMMINGES
E·G·863,871

E4
COMMINGES
EG·853

E6
-600 BOLOGNA
M·I·85

E7
FINISTERRE
DF2, 700

E8
-100?
SWISS BMCE

E9
-100?
SWISS   BMCE

F2
NORBA
N·S·1904·416
FALERII
M·I·319·4
SPARTA·ABS·1907·111

F3
-550 APULIA
M·AP·30·2

F4
-700 CUMA
MA1913·XLII

F5
CERVETRI
M·I· 332·1

F6
E·APPENN?
M·I·159·16

F8
-700? VERRUCCHIO
NS1898,350

F9
-600? NESACTIUM
11 KM, NE, POLA
JOAI 1903
B& 70

G9
HITTITE, M·S·IV

G1
700 ATHENS
K·B·III

G2
MESEMBRIA
M·S·E·52

G22
MMIII
SEAL
EPM·372
TROY·SI·1999

G3
-900 BR
HALLSTATT
R.V. V·XXII

G4
MM1·
PLATANOS
X·M·XIV

G5
TROY
S·I·1862

G6
CHEITAN DAGH
CAUCASUS
MCA·179

G7
HELLENENDORF
TRANSCAUCASIA
CA119

G74
BR
KO BAN
MAK.XVII

G8
BISMIYA BIS
BANKS·386

G94
TEPE
MUSSIAN
MAK·903

G98
JAPAN
MSE·V·

J2
CLONMACNOISE
+1000? CCO,9C

J3
-140 NUMANTIA
E·N·XXXIV

J4
-140 NUMANTIA
E·N·XL

J5
FE·I· WURTEMBURG
CAF 45

J6
-10?
LONDON,SHIELD,R·C·A·159

J7
+400?HEYDEKRUG
E·PRUSSIA
RV·IX· CCXXXVII

J8
+400 YORK,xlviii
BAE II

K2
LATIUM
M·I·14 L·19

K3
APULIA
-600 R·M·I·222
" XLiV
BONN,R·S·XiX I

K4
-1150 ITALY
M·C· 6·6

K5
MM·I PORTI
X·M·viii

K6
TROY
S·I·1868

K8
MED ZAHRAN
(EL UBAID)
B·U· 87

L2
CRETAN, IVORY. M·S·54

L3
STEPAN-ZMINDA
BELT-END C·C·I·LV

L4
BR·TRANSCAUCAS.
ON JAR.
Z·E· 1905, 148

L5
FE·I· BRONZE AXE
UPPER KOBAN
OSSETIA   C·C·I·i.

L7
PERSIA
M·S·E·V

L8
CHINA
M·S·E·64

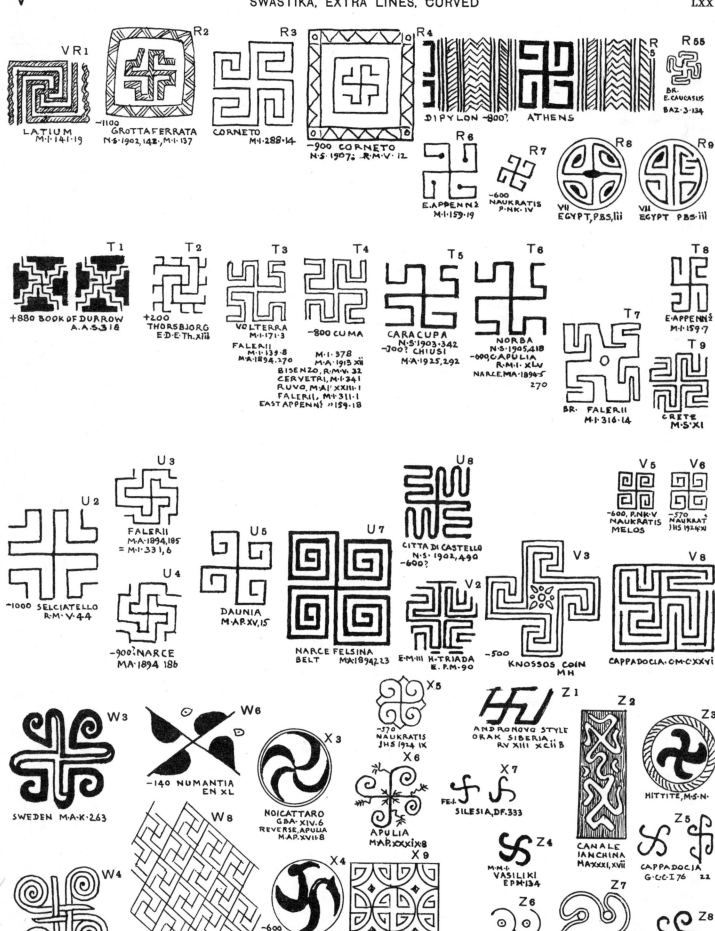

VR1 — LATIUM M·I·141·19

R2 — GROTTAFERRATA ~1100 N·S·1902,142; M·I·137

R3 — CORNETO M·I·288·14

R4 — ~900 CORNETO N·S·1907; R·M·V·12

R — DIPYLON ~800? ATHENS

R5

R55 — BR. E.CAUCASUS BAZ·3·134

R6 — E.APPENN? M·I·159·19

R7 — ~600 NAUKRATIS P·NK·IV

R8 — VII EGYPT, P.BS.lii

R9 — VII EGYPT P.BS·iii

T1 — +880 BOOK OF DURROW A.A.S.318

T2 — +200 THORSBJORG E·D·E·Th.xIii

T3 — VOLTERRA M·I·171·3 FALERII M·I·139·8 M·A·1894.270 BISENZO, R·M·V· 32 CERVETRI, M·I·341 RUVO, M·AI'XXIII·I FALERII, M·I·311·1 EAST APPENN? »159·18

T4 — ~800 CUMA M·I·378 M·A·1913 XII

T5 — CARACUPA N·S·1903·342 ~700? CHIUSI M·A·1925,292

T6 — NORBA N·S·1905.418 ~600 CAPULIA R·M·I·XLV NARCE.MA·1894·5 270

T7 — BR. FALERII M·I·316·14

T8 — E.APPENN? M·I·159·7

T9 — CRETE M·S·XI

U2 — ~1000 SELCIATELLO R·M·V·44

U3 — FALERII M·A·1894,185 = M·I·331,6

U4 — ~900? NARCE MA·1894 186

U5 — DAUNIA M·A·P·XV,15

U7 — NARCE FELSINA BELT MA·1894,223

U8 — CITTA DI CASTELLO N·S·1902,490 ~600?

V2 — E·M·III H.TRIADA E. P.M·90

V3 — ~500 KNOSSOS COIN MH

V5 — ~600, P.NK·V NAUKRATIS MELOS

V6 — ~570 NAUKRAT? JHS 1924 XI

V8 — CAPPADOCIA·OM·C·XXVI

W3 — SWEDEN M·A·K·263

W6 — ~140 NUMANTIA EN XL

W8 — TENEI MARNE HELMET, DF2 490

W4 — +1100 CONCHAN MANX CROSS X·62

X3 — NOICATTARO GBA·XIV.6 REVERSE, APULIA M·A·P·XVII·8

X4 — ~600 M?SANNACE GBA·III·6 PEUKETIA M·A·P·XXIV,3a

X5 — ~570 NAUKRATIS JHS 1924 IX

X6 — APULIA M·A·P·XXXIX·8

X7 — FE·I SILESIA, DF.333

X9 — +500 RAVENNA MA-1916·753

Z1 — ANDRONOVO STYLE ORAK SIBERIA RV XIII XCii B

Z2 — CANALE IANCHINA MAXXXI,XVII

Z3 — HITTITE, M·S·N.

Z4 — M·M·I VASILIKI EPM·134

Z5 — CAPPADOCIA G·C·C·I 76 22

Z6 — CRETE EPM·II·107

Z7 — CRETE EPM II·107

Z8 — LEH. M·S·E·vi

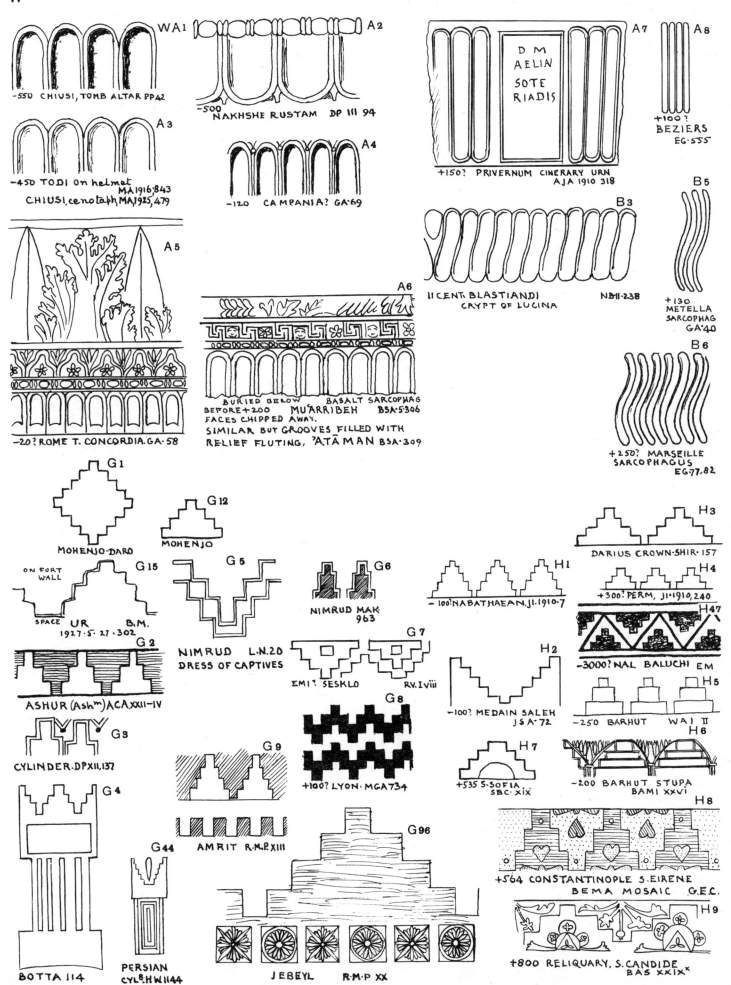

WA1
−550 CHIUSI, TOMB ALTAR PP 42

A3
−450 TODI on helmet MA 1916, 843
CHIUSI, cenotaph MA 1925, 479

A2
−500 NAKHSHE RUSTAM DP III 94

A4
−120 CAMPANIA? GA·69

A7
+150? PRIVERNUM CINERARY URN AJA 1910 318
D M AELIN SOTE RIADIS

A8
+100? BEZIERS EG·555

A5

A6
BURIED BELOW BASALT SARCOPHAG
BEFORE +200 MU'ARRIBEH BSA·5306
FACES CHIPPED AWAY.
SIMILAR BUT GROOVES FILLED WITH
RELIEF FLUTING, 'ATĀMAN BSA·309

−20? ROME T. CONCORDIA. GA·58

B3
II CENT. BLASTIANDI NB II·238
CRYPT OF LUCINA

B5
+130 METELLA SARCOPHAG GA·40

B6
+250? MARSEILLE SARCOPHAGUS EG·77, 82

G1
MOHENJO-DARO

G12
MOHENJO

G15
ON FORT WALL
SPACE UR B.M.
1927·5·27·302

G2
ASHUR (Ash^m) ACA XXII-IV

G3
CYLINDER. DP XII, 137

G4
BOTTA 114

G44
PERSIAN CYL & HW II 144

G5
NIMRUD L.N. 20
DRESS OF CAPTIVES

G6
NIMRUD MAK· 963

G7
EM I? SESKLO RV. I viii

G8
+100? LYON. MGA 734

G9

G96

AMRIT R.M.P XIII

JEBEYL R.M.P XX

H1
−100? NABATHAEAN. JI·1910·7

H2
−100? MEDAIN SALEH JSA·72

H3
DARIUS CROWN·SHIR·157

H4
+300? PERM, JI·1910, 240

H47
−3000? NAL BALUCHI EM

H5
−250 BARHUT WAI II

H6
−200 BARHUT STUPA BAMI XXVI

H7
+535 S·SOFIA SBC·xix

H8
+564 CONSTANTINOPLE S·EIRENE
BEMA MOSAIC G.E.C.

H9
+800 RELIQUARY, S. CANDIDE BAS XXIX^x

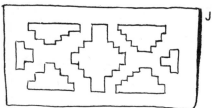

+600 HEJNUM GOTLAND
OPEN WORK   NSO 40

J3

LOT ET GARONNE. AFW
coarse SARAGOSSA   82

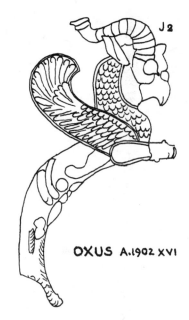

J2

OXUS A. 1902 XVI

J4

W. SWITZERLAND
GARNET. AFW. 102

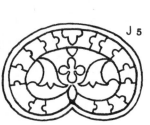

GOTHIC. ITALY. AGL. 13
GARNET IN GOLD

J7

BR. NARIASSOVA
MM XXX

J6

WURTEMBURG
GARNET. AFW. 115

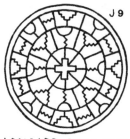

LOMBARD BELLUNO
GARNET   AGL 128

CAUCASUS AFW. 3
GARNET BOSS

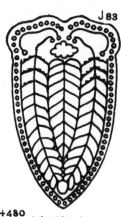

J83

+480 CHILDERIC
AFW 62
C.A.C. p.104

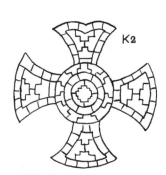

K2

+650 IXWORTH, AAS. 259

K4

+700   MLG 211
LINDIS FARNE

K5

+700 LINDISFARNE
BAE. V. XXXIV

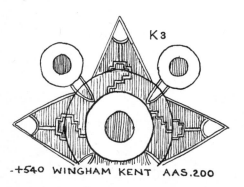

K3

+540 WINGHAM KENT AAS. 200

K7

TIBETAN W. OF PEKIN   BCA. 14   L
4 STEP HONAN·BCAXL· 6 STEP SZECHUAN

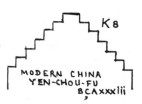

K8

MODERN CHINA
YEN-CHOU-FU
BCAXxxiii

K9

FRANKFORT TOWN-HALL Φ

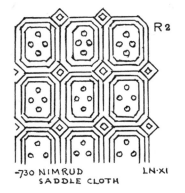

R2

-730 NIMRUD
SADDLE CLOTH   LN·XI

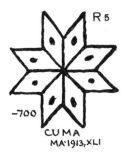

R5

-700
CUMA
MA·1913, XLI

R6

+500? RIFEH
P&R, XXXVII 8

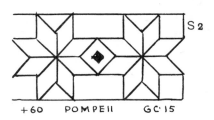

R8

SARDINIA, ALGHERO
NS·1904·333

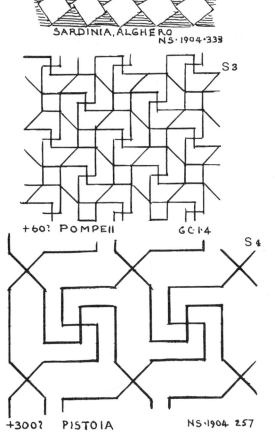

S3

+60? POMPEII   GC·14

S4

+300? PISTOIA   NS·1904 257

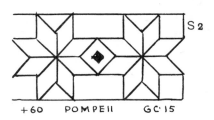

S2

+60   POMPEII   GC·15

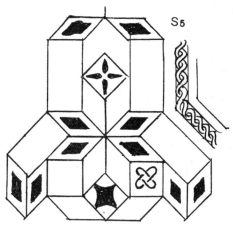

S5

ROME, VIA TUSCOLANA.   NS·1905·72

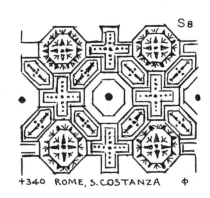

S8

+340 ROME, S.COSTANZA   Φ

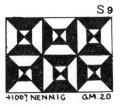

S9

+100? NENNIG   GM.20

T1

+400
RAVENNA
HONORIUS   MA·1916·766

T2

+500 RAVENNA
THEODORIC   MA·1916,759

T3

+500 RAVENNA
THEODORIC   MA·1916·758

T5

+500 RAVENNA   MA·1916·751
THEODORIC

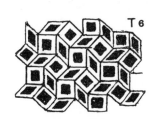

T6

+500 RAVENNA
THEODORIC MA·1916·790

T7

+800 GOSPEL OF
CHARLEMAGNE
AJA 1920 152

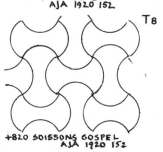

T8

+820 SOISSONS GOSPEL
AJA 1920 152

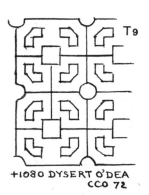

T9

+1080 DYSERT O'DEA
CCO 72

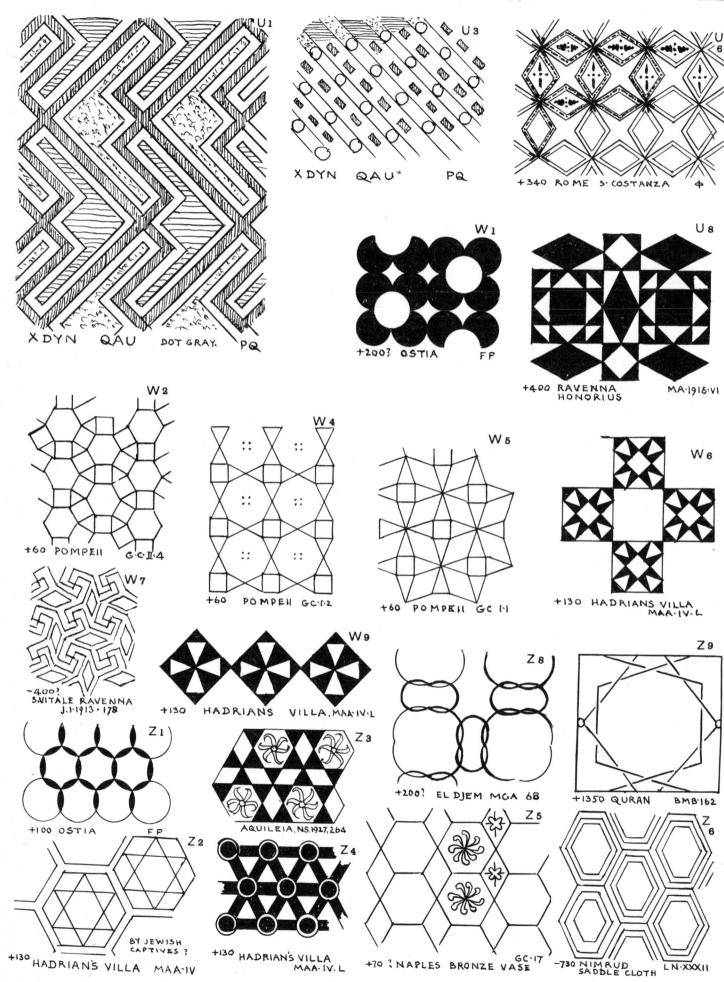

U1 X DYN QAU PQ

U3 X DYN QAU" PQ

U6 +340 ROME S·COSTANZA φ

W1 +200? OSTIA FP

U8 +400 RAVENNA HONORIUS MA·1915·VI

W2 +60 POMPEII GC·II·4

W4 +60 POMPEII GC·I·2

W5 +60 POMPEII GC·I·I

W6 +130 HADRIANS VILLA MAA·IV·L

W7 −400? S.VITALE RAVENNA J·I·1913·178

W9 +130 HADRIANS VILLA, MAA·IV·L

Z8 +200? EL DJEM MGA 6B

Z9 +1350 QURAN BMB·162

Z1 +100 OSTIA FP

Z3 AQUILEIA. NS.1927, 264

Z2 BY JEWISH CAPTIVES? +130 HADRIAN'S VILLA MAA·IV

Z4 +130 HADRIAN'S VILLA MAA·IV·L

Z5 +70? NAPLES BRONZE VASE GC·I7

Z6 −730 NIMRUD SADDLE CLOTH LN·XXXII

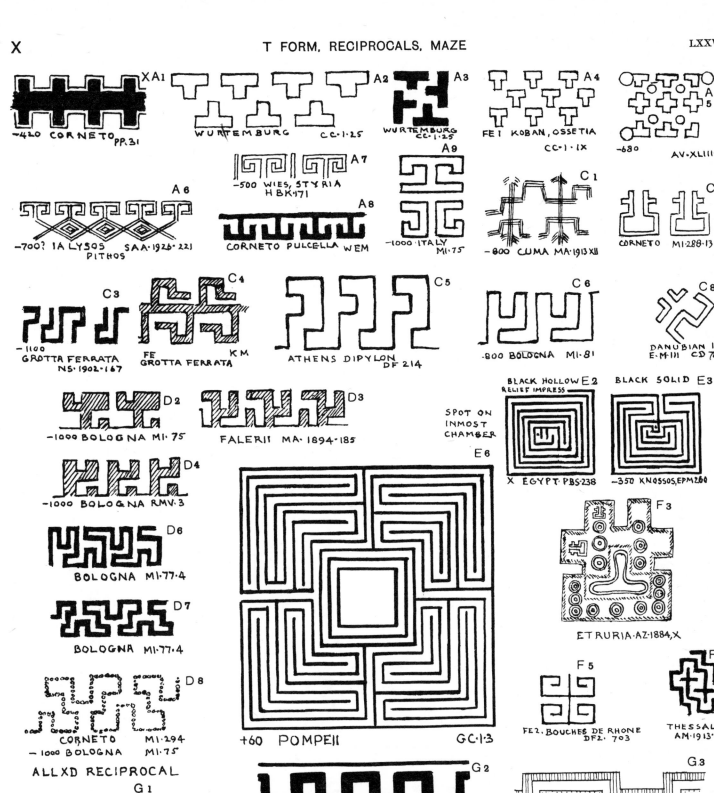

XA1

-420 CORNETO PP.31

WÜRTEMBURG   CC·1·25   A2

WÜRTEMBURG CC·1·25   A3

FE 1 KOBAN, OSSETIA   A4
CC·1·IX

A5
-680   AV·XLIII·2

A7
-500 WIES, STYRIA
H BK·171

A9

A6
-700? IALYSOS   SAA·1926·221
PITHOS

A8
CORNETO PULCELLA   WEM

-1000 ·ITALY
MI·75

C1
-800 CUMA MA·1913 XII

C2
CORNETO   MI·288·13

C3
-1100
GROTTA FERRATA
NS·1902·167

C4
FE
GROTTA FERRATA   KM

C5
ATHENS DIPYLON
DF 214

C6
-800 BOLOGNA MI·81

C8
DANUBIAN I
E·M·III   CD 78

D2
-1000 BOLOGNA MI·75

D3
FALERII MA·1894·185

BLACK HOLLOW E2
RELIEF IMPRESS

BLACK SOLID E3

SPOT ON
INMOST
CHAMBER
E6

X EGYPT PBS·238   -350 KNOSSOS, EPM 260

D4
-1000 BOLOGNA RMV·3

D6
BOLOGNA MI·77·4

F3
ETRURIA·AZ·1884·X

D7
BOLOGNA MI·77·4

D8
CORNETO   MI·294
-1000 BOLOGNA   MI·75

ALL XD RECIPROCAL

F5
FE2, BOUCHES DE RHONE
DF2· 703

F7
THESSALY
AM·1913·29

+60 POMPEII   GC·1·3

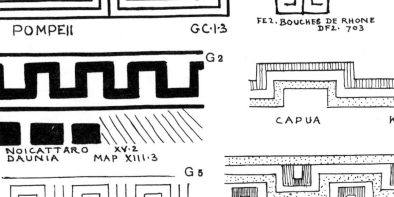

G1
-700 CUMA
RMI· 35

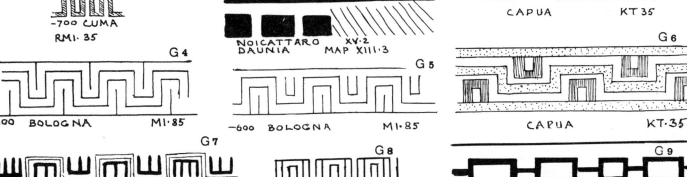

G2

NOICATTARO   XV·2
DAUNIA   MAP XIII·3

G3
CAPUA   KT 35

G6
CAPUA   KT·35

G4
-600 BOLOGNA   MI·85

G5
-600 BOLOGNA   MI·85

G7
-680 CENTRAL APULIA   GBA·II·1
-600 MONTE SANNACE

G8
KAMEIROS. ABS·1906·72

G9
APULIA MAP·I 2   DAUNIA MAP·XII·14

+440   RAVENNA   PLACIDIA   XK2   φ

FE·I· NANCY   DF 219   K5
HAUTE MARNE DF 247

K7
SEE
LX8

CLONMACNOISE   CCO 7B

L2
—600 S·APULIA
RM1·45

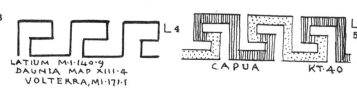

L3
—500   ESTE BRONZE STUDS
R·M1· 4·5

L4
LATIUM M·I·140·9
DAUNIA MAP XIII·4
VOLTERRA, MI·171·1

L5
CAPUA   KT·40

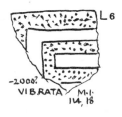

L6
—2000?
VIBRATA M·I·
14, 18

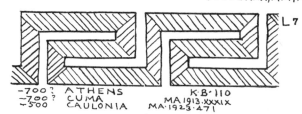

—700? ATHENS   L7
—700? CUMA   MA 1913.XXXIX
—500   CAULONIA   MA·1923·471

L8
—800 BOLOGNA RMV·7

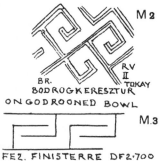

L9
—600 BOLOGNA   M1·85

M6

XDYN   QAU   PQ

M7
—600   ESTE   MA 1887·137

M2
RV
II
TOKAY
BR.
BODROGKERESZTUR
ON GODROONED BOWL

M.3

FEZ. FINISTERRE DF2·700

M8

XDYN   QAU   PQ

M 4

CLONMACNOISE
CCO·7A

M5
—600 BOLOGNA   MI·85
RAVENNA, S.APOL·N· MAP XXVII

N3
CAPUA   KT· 33

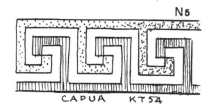

N5
CAPUA   KT 54

O3
VALENZANO
GBA·XII·5

O6
MID APULIA
MAP. XIX O

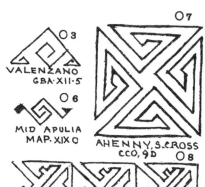

O7

AHENNY, S.CROSS
CCO.9D   O8

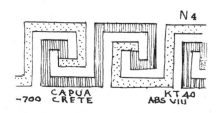

N4
—700 CAPUA
CRETE   KT40
ABS VIII

N8
+520 RAVENNA S·APOL·NUOV· φ

+924 MONASTERBOICE   CCO 7G
MUIRDACH

XP2

CERVETRI   MI·340·4

-700   ATHENS   KB 110

P3

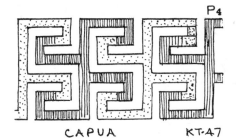

P4

CAPUA   KT·47

P6

-700?   ATHENS   A2·1884 IX

P7

HALLSTATT   BC 57

P8

HALLSTATT, SCABBARD BC·57

P9

-600   ESTE BRONZE STUDS. MA 1897.139.

   T1

RHODES. KB 114.

   T2

KARIA, HU II, 246

-600?

   T3

+800?
CROPTHORNE
CROSS HEAD
BEQ 38

T4

VALENZANO, GBA·IX.3

   T5

CAMBRIDGE
A.1925,245

   T6

-670 CAERE RME₄

T7

+1080 CCO.56
DYSERT O'DEA

DIAGONAL
AT FERNS

   T8

MEIGLE   RCA 286

   T9

CARDONAGH, CCO.51

U2

-500 ATHENS DRESS   φ

U3

-450   SYRACUSE

   U4

N·CHINA SCREEN. BCA
ALSO RHOMBIC CLXIII

   U5

+100? AIX PROVENCE
MGA·47

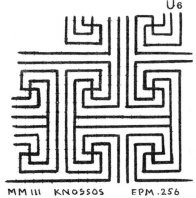   U6

MM III   KNOSSOS   EPM.256

   U7

+440 RAVENNA, PLACIDIA   φ

   U8

+440   RAVENNA, PLACIDIA
N B·II·152

   U9

+101 IS-SANAMEN   BSA·5·XIX

CAPUA　　　　　　　KT 53

+200 INKHIL
+60 POMPEII　　　　　　BSA·5·286,314
　　　　　　　　　　　　　GC·II·3

+500? RIFEH　　PGR·XXXVII B

CAPUA　　　　　　　KT 40

BAWYT　　　　　　GCCIII

CAPUA　　　　　　　KT·55

-700 RHODES　　K·B·115

+200 OXYRHYNKHOS COLONNADE

PTC·XXXV

-300 CALTAGIRONE　　MA·1922·117

-500 LANUVIUM
MA 1921·322

-600 NAUKRATIS
POLEMARKHOS　　PNK·IV

-570 DAFNEH　PD·XXXII

-500 CAULONIA MA·1923,440

VULCI　　　　DA 188
C·METELLA　　GA 60
CAPUA　　　　KT 53

+40? VASE　　　　　GA 49

-500 CAULONIA　　MA 1923,442
+500 OXYRHYNKHOS PTC XLVII

CAPUA KT·53

-600 MONTE SANNACE GBA LIV

XII DYN SIUT　　MS·71

-600 MONTE SANNACE, GBA pl.IV

ESTE II NESACTIUM ISTRIA
RV·VIII cl

-600? PRAESOS
ABS·1906·50

-600
Mt SANNACE
GBA·V·3

Z 56

JDE·38

-650 KOBAN UPPER OSSETIA CC·I·XX"

MÄHREN MBH,1912,59

SIEBENBÜRGEN　ZE·1907·115

AEGINA
AZ·1882·IX

NEO MEZINE
RV·XIII,XVI -50 GLASTONBURY
BGG LXXXVI

BULGARIA　　MS·85

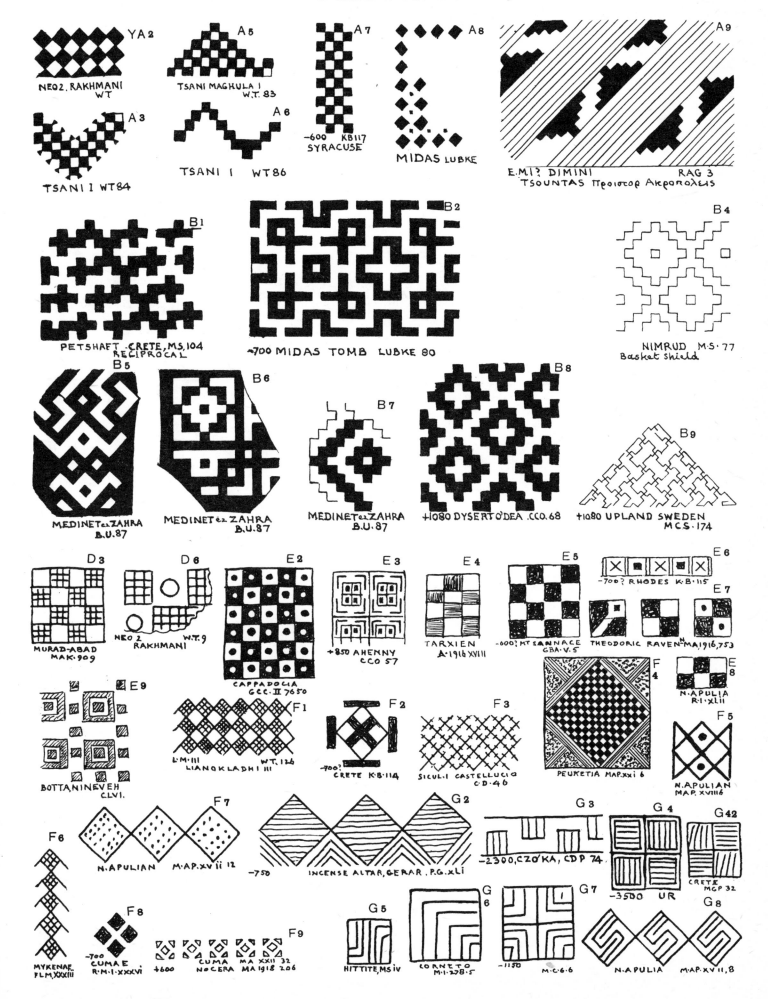

YA2 NEO2. RAKHMANI WT

A5 TSANI MAGHULA I W.T. 83

A7 -600 KB117 SYRACUSE

A8 MIDAS LUBKE

A9

A3 TSANI I WT84

A6 TSANI I WT86

E.MI? DIMINI RAG 3
TSOUNTAS Προιστορ Ακροπολεις

B1 PETSHAFT CRETE, MS. 104 RECIPROCAL

B2 ~700 MIDAS TOMB LUBKE 80

B4 NIMRUD M.S. 77 Basket shield

B5 MEDINET ez ZAHRA B.U. 87

B6 MEDINET ez ZAHRA B.U. 87

B7 MEDINET ez ZAHRA B.U. 87

B8 +1080 DYSERTO'DEA .CCO. 68

B9 +1080 UPLAND SWEDEN MCS. 174

D3 MURAD-ABAD MAK. 909

D6 NEO 2 RAKHMANI W.T. 9

E2 CAPPADOCIA G.C.C. II 7650

E3 +850 AHENNY CCO 57

E4 TARXIEN A. 1916 XVIII

E5 -000? MT SANNACE GBA. V. 5

E6 -700? RHODES K.B. 115

E7 THEODORIC RAVEN MA 1916, 753

E9 BOTTANINEVEH CLVI.

F1 L.M. III LIANOKLADHI III W.T. 126

F2 -700? CRETE K.B. 114

F3 SICULI CASTELLUCIO C.D. 46

F4 PEUKETIA MAP. xxi 6

E8 N. APULIA R.I. XLII

F5 N. APULIAN MAP. XVIII 6

F6 MYKENAE FLM XXXIII

F7 N. APULIAN M. AP. XV ii 12

F8 -700 CUMAE R. M. I. XXXVI

F9 +600 CUMA NOCERA CUMA MA XXII 32 MA 1918 206

G2 -750 INCENSE ALTAR, GERAR. P.G. xLi

G3 -2300, CZO'KA, CDP 74

G4 -3500 UR

G42 CRETE MGP 32

G5 HITTITE, MS iv

G6 CORNETO M. I. 278. 5

G7 -1150 M.C.6.6

G8 N. APULIA MAP. XV II, 8

YH2 I dyn. ARMLET, P.R.T. II Vi

H3 NEOL. PATERNO CATANIA M·A·1914 V

H4 -1400 IALYSOS FLM. iii

H5 -700 RHODES K·B·115

H6 -500 N.APULIA   R·I· xLiii

H7 -700? CRETE K·B·114

H8 N.APULIA, R·I· xLiii

J2 -2300 CZÓKA, CDP 74

J6 LATIUM M·I·141·16

J4 NORBA M·A·1905,148

J.7 -600 SYRACUSE M·A·1918,490

L.2 N.APULIAN MA P.XVII 10

L3 +350 AHENNY, CCO, 69

L -600? MT SANNACE GBA·VI·6

L6 -600? MT. SANNACE GBA·V

L8 ANT.R.

L9 ANT.R.

M2 MMI· PLATANOS XM·xiii

M3 MMI. PLATANOS XM·xiv

M5 HITTITE H.H. 212

M7 -1400? IALYSOS GLASS. SAA·1924, 93

M8 -700? KOPENHAGEN K·B·112

M9 -700? CYPRUS K·B·114

N2 -570 NAUKRATIS JHS·1924 XI

N4 -800 CHIUSI MA·1925,434

N5 THEODORIC RAVENN MA 1918 753

N7 +700 HARTLEPOOL BAE V, vi

N8 +800   CCO p.19 CLONMACNOISE

O1 TEPE MUSSIAN MA K,897

O11 MOHENJO-DARO

O13 FALERII M·I·322·J

O2 FE BISENZIO KM

O24 YORUBA ESA·V

O27 CORNETO M·A·1905,678

O3 NORBA N.S.1904,416

O4 O5 NORBA N·S·1904,416 NIMES EG 682·7

O6 -600? KARIA HU II 246

O7 CRETE, M·S·X

O8 FE BISENZIO KM

O9 -900 BISENZIO M·I·257

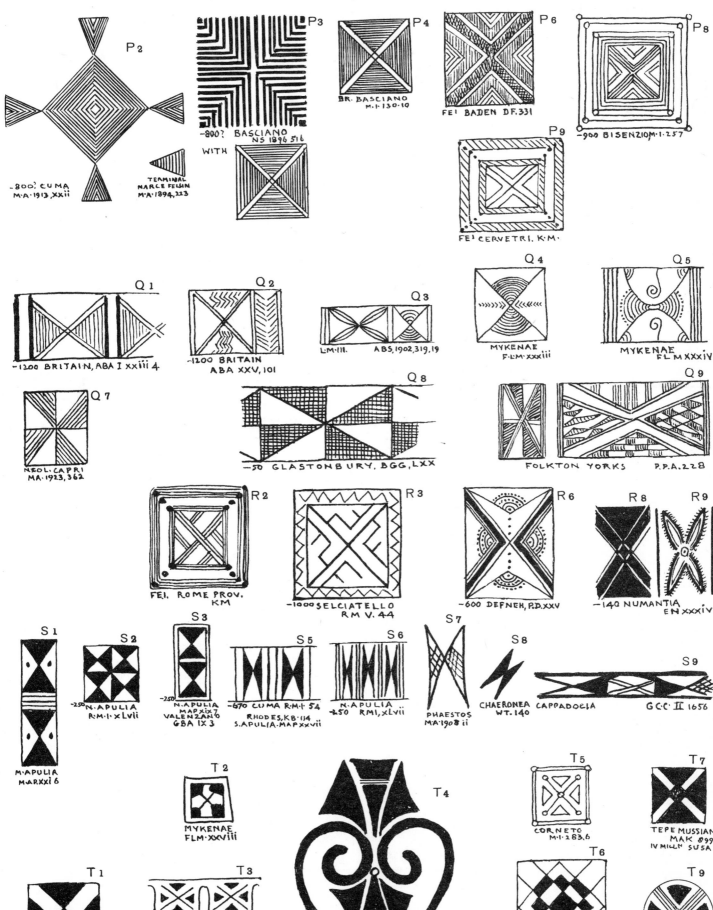

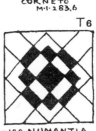

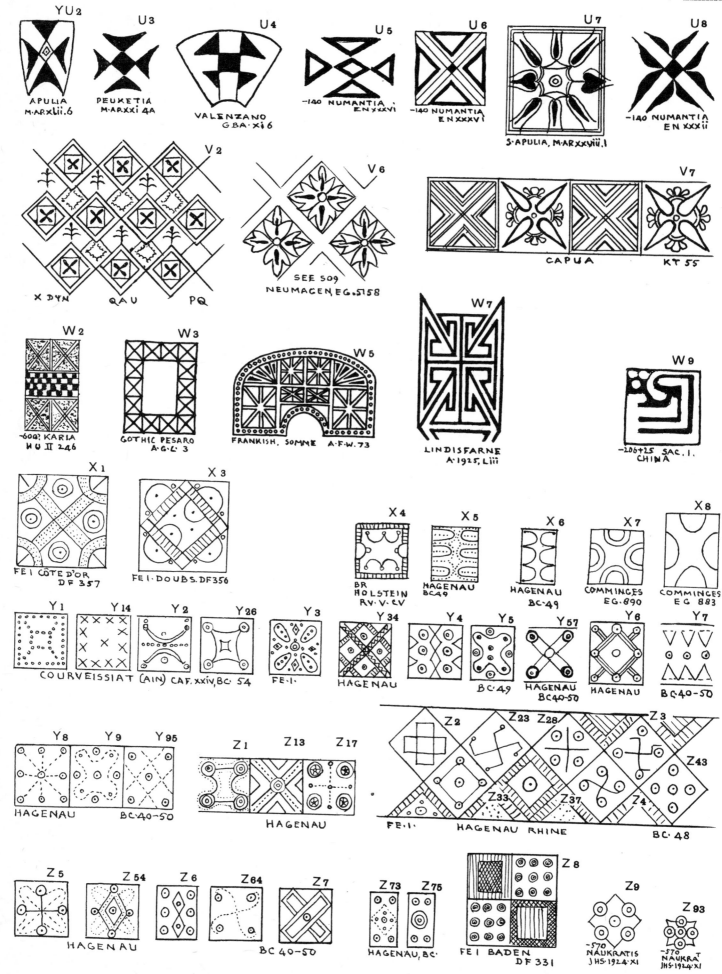

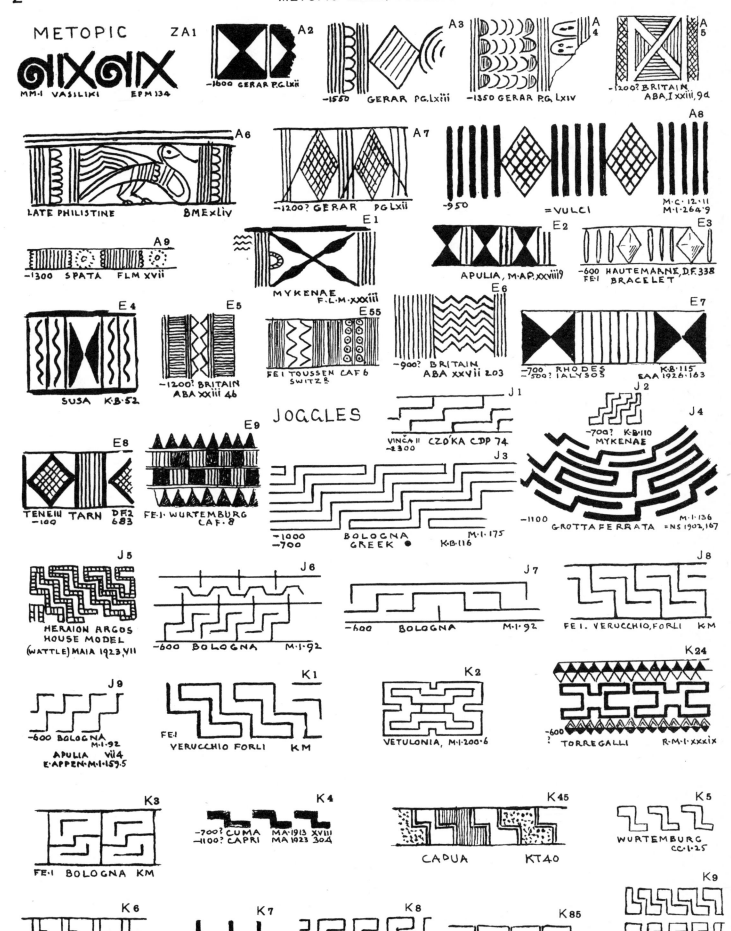

P 1
-550? IALYSOS　　SAA·1926·161

P.2
APULIA　　MAP.I.2

P 3
DAUNIA
LATIUM
-700? RHODES　　MAP XIII·7
MI·141·14
KB·114

P 4
EM. KALATHIANA, SEAL. EPM.II·26

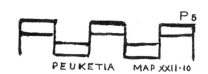

P 5
PEUKETIA　　MAP XXII·10

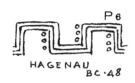

P 6
HAGENAU　　BC·48

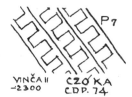

P 7
VINČA II
-2300　　CZOKA CDP. 74

P 8
PRE-INCA BOWL CHIMU PERU

P 9
-700? CRETE　　KB·114

V 3
N·APULIA MAP. XVII.8

V 4
GOTHIC, SWEDEN AFW 16

V 7
-700? THERA KB·114

V 8
+500 RAVENNA MA·1916 753

V 9
MODERN
FENCE SZECHUAN BCA·CXI

P 92
ANDRONOVO STYLE　ORAK SIBERIA RV·XIII·XCIIB

W 1
-1300 IALYSOS SAA·1926 #80

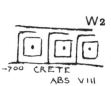

W 2
-700 CRETE ABS VIII

W 3
BR. E·APENNINE MI·130·5

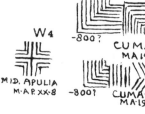

W 4
MID. APULIA M·AP XX·8

W 5
-800? CUMA MA 1913 XII

W 6
-800? CUMA MA 1913 XVIII

W 7
GOTHIC BAVARIA AFW·110

W 8
GOTHIC TURIN AGL·63

W 9
BARBERINI MAA 1925 p.62

X 2
-3500 UR

X 3
-3500 UR

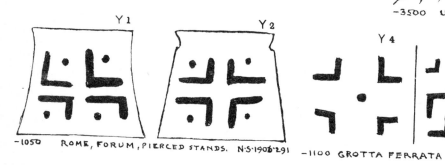

Y 1　　　　　　Y 2
-1050 ROME, FORUM, PIERCED STANDS. N·S·1906·291

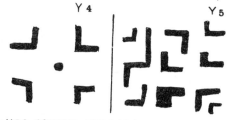

Y 4　　　　　Y 5
-1100 GROTTA FERRATA　　NS·1902·185

Y 8
CORNETO　MI·290·2

Y 9
FALERII　MI·320·13

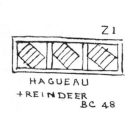

Z 1
HAGUEAU
+REINDEER BC 48

Z 2
LM·III WT·125
LIANOKLADHI·III

Z 3
NEO· CAPRI MA·1923·i

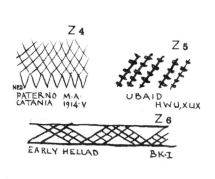

Z 4
NEO
PATERNO M·A CATANIA 1914·V

Z 5
UBAID HWU,XUX

Z 6
EARLY HELLAD　BK·I

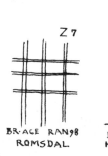

Z 7
BR·AGE RAN98 ROMSDAL

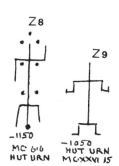

Z 8
-1150 MC 6·6 HUT URN

Z 9
-1050 HUT URN MC·XXVI 15

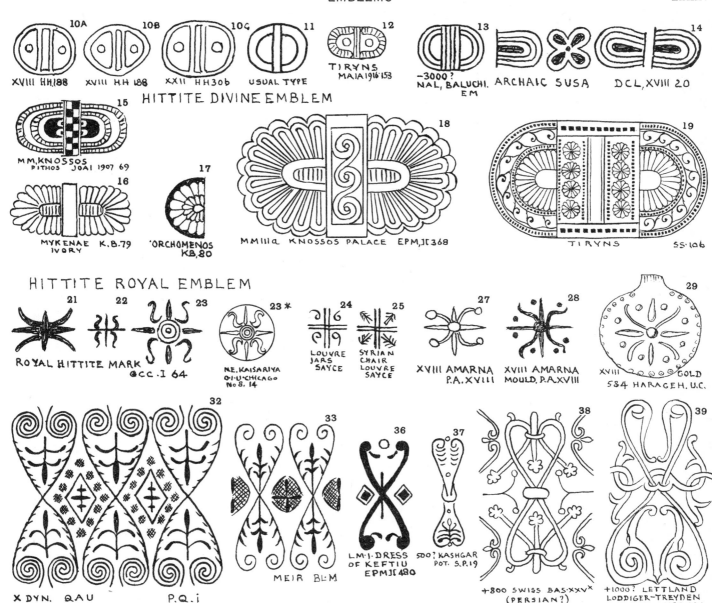

10A — XVIII HH.188
10B — XVIII HH.188
10C — XXII HH30b
11 — USUAL TYPE
12 — TIRYNS MAIA 1916·153
13 — -3000? NAL, BALUCHI. EM
ARCHAIC SUSA
14 — DCL, XVIII 20

HITTITE DIVINE EMBLEM

15 — MM, KNOSSOS PITHOS JOAI 1907 69
16 — MYKENAE IVORY K.B.79
17 — 'ORCHOMENOS KB, 80
18 — MMIIIa KNOSSOS PALACE EPM, II 368
19 — TIRYNS SS·106

HITTITE ROYAL EMBLEM

21 — ROYAL HITTITE MARK
22
23 — GCC. I 64
23* — N.E. KAISARIYA O·I·U·CHICAGO No 8. 14
24 — LOUVRE JARS SAYCE
25 — SYRIAN CHAIR LOUVRE SAYCE
27 — XVIII AMARNA P.A. XVIII
28 — XVIII AMARNA MOULD. P.A. XVIII
29 — XVIII 584 HARAGEH. U.C. GOLD

32 — X DYN. QAU   P.Q. i
33 — MEIR BL·M
36 — LM·I· DRESS OF KEFTIU EPM·II 480
37 — 500? KASHGAR POT. S.P. 19
38 — +800 SWISS BAS·XXV× (PERSIAN?)
39 — +1000? LETTLAND LODDIGER-TREYDEN NSO 104

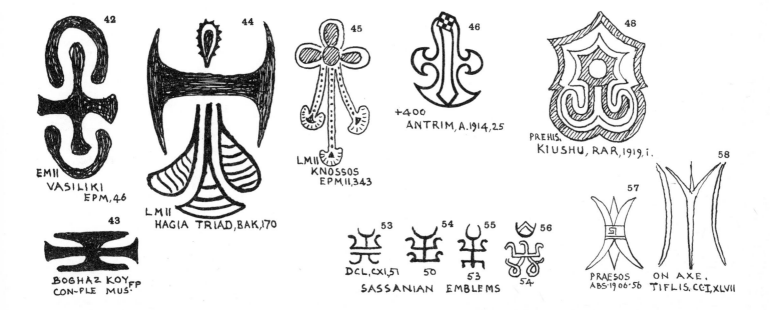

42 — EM II VASILIKI EPM, 46
43 — BOGHAZ KOY CON-PLE MUS· FP
44 — LM II HAGIA TRIAD, BAK, 170
45 — LM II KNOSSOS EPM, II, 343
46 — +400 ANTRIM, A. 1914, 25
48 — PREHIS. KIUSHU, RAR, 1919, i.
53 — DCL, CXI, 57   50
54
55 — 53
56
SASSANIAN EMBLEMS
57 — PRAESOS ABS·1906·56
58 — ON AXE. TIFLIS. CCI, XLVII

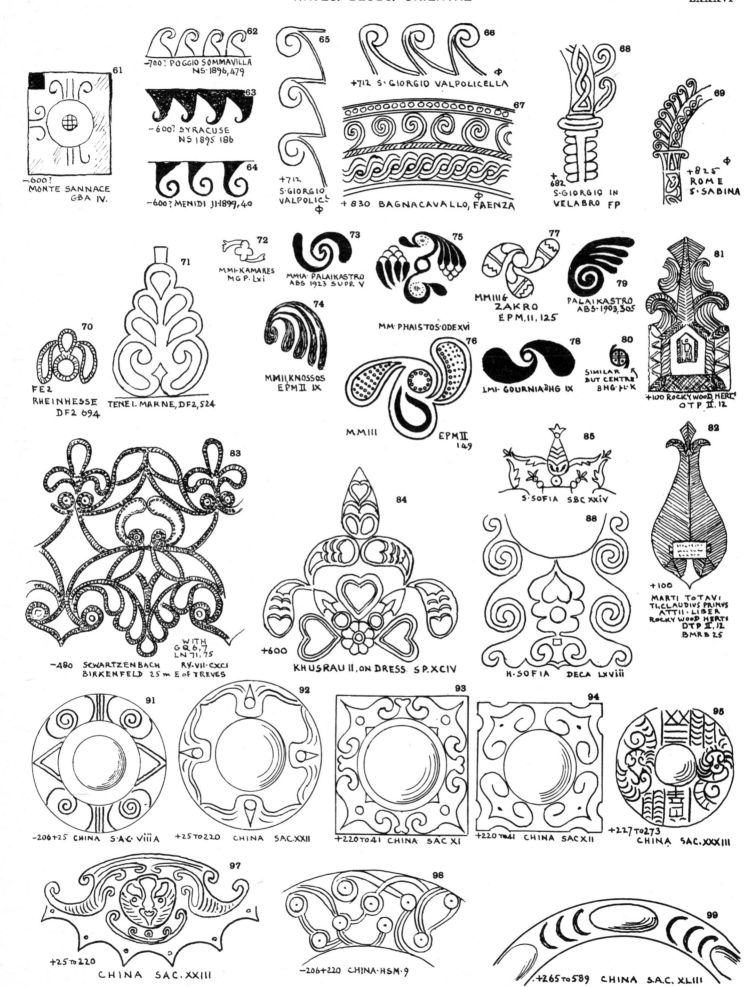

61 -600?
MONTE SANNACE
G.B.A. IV.

62 -700? POGGIO SOMMAVILLA
NS·1896,479

63 -600? SYRACUSE
NS 1895 186

64 -600? MENIDI JH·1899, 40

65 +712
S·GIORGIO
VALPOLIC.

66 +712 S·GIORGIO VALPOLICELLA

67 +830 BAGNACAVALLO, FAENZA

68 +682
S·GIORGIO IN
VELABRO FP

69 +825
ROME
S·SABINA

70 FE2
RHEINHESSE
DF2 694

71 TENEI. MARNE, DF2, 524

72 MMI·KAMARES
MGP·Lxi

73 MMIA·PALAIKASTRO
ABS 1923 SUPR·V

74 MMII, KNOSSOS
EPM II IX

75 MM·PHAISTOS·ODE XVI

76 MMIII   EPM II
149

77 MMIIIG
ZAKRO
E.P.M.II, 125

78 LMI· GOURNIA BHG IX

79 PALAIKASTRO
ABS·1903,305

80 SIMILAR
BUT CENTRE
BHG·II·K

81 +100 ROCKY WOOD HERTS
OTP II. 12

82 +100
MARTI TOTAVI
TI.CLAUDIUS PRIMVS
ATTII·LIBER
ROCKY WOOD HERTS
OTP II. 12
BMRB 25

83 -480 SCWARTZENBACH
BIRKENFELD 25 m E of TREVES
WITH
GQ 6,7
LN 71,75
RY·VII·CXCI

84 +600 KHUSRAU II. ON DRESS SP·XCIV

85 S·SOFIA SBC XXiv

88 H·SOFIA   DECA LXViii

91 -206+25 CHINA S·A·C·Viiia

92 +25 TO 220 CHINA SAC·XXII

93 +220 TO 41 CHINA SAC XI

94 +220 TO 41 CHINA SAC XII

95 +227 TO 273 CHINA SAC·XXXIII

97 +25 TO 220 CHINA SAC·XXIII

98 -206+220 CHINA·HSM·9

99 +265 TO 589 CHINA S.A.C. XLIII

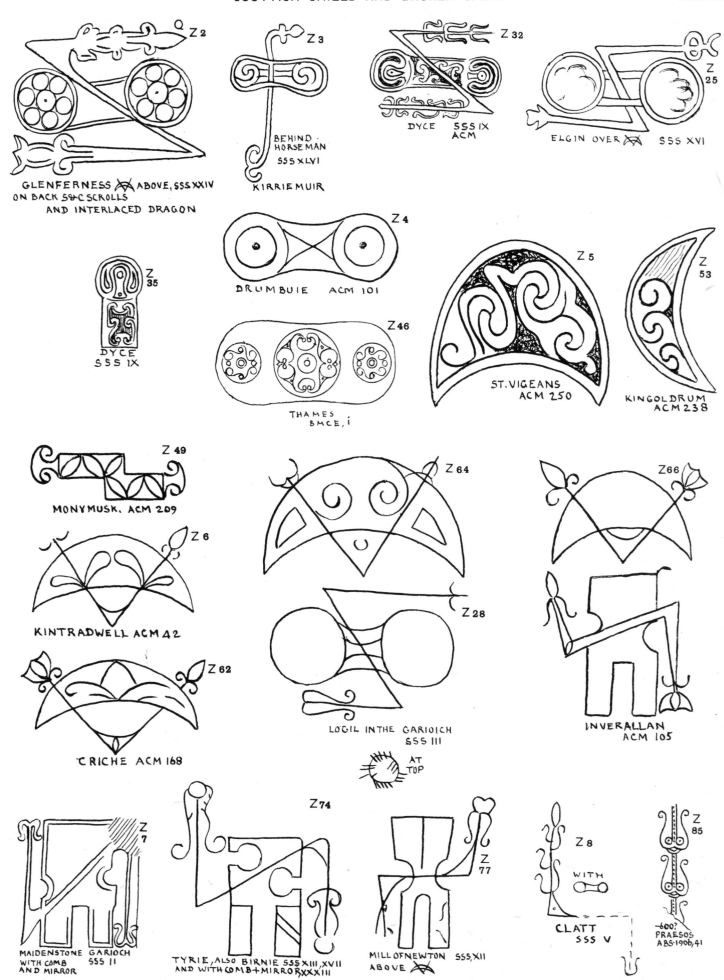

Q Z2
GLENFERNESS ⨉ ABOVE, SSS XXIV
ON BACK S&C SCROLLS
AND INTERLACED DRAGON

Z3
BEHIND·
HORSEMAN
SSS XLVI
KIRRIEMUIR

Z32
DYCE SSS IX
ACM

Z25
ELGIN OVER ⨉⨉   SSS XVI

Z35
DYCE
SSS IX

Z4
DRUMBUIE   ACM 101

Z46
THAMES
BMCE, i

Z5
ST. VIGEANS
ACM 250

Z53
KINGOLDRUM
ACM 238

Z49
MONYMUSK, ACM 209

Z64

Z66

Z6
KINTRADWELL ACM 42

Z28
LOGIL IN THE GARIOCH
SSS III

INVERALLAN
ACM 105

Z62
CRICHE ACM 168

AT
TOP

Z7
MAIDENSTONE GARIOCH
WITH COMB
AND MIRROR   SSS II

Z74
TYRIE, ALSO BIRNIE SSS XIII, XVII
AND WITH COMB+MIRROR XXXIII

Z77
MILL OF NEWTON   SSS XII
ABOVE ⨉⨉

Z8
WITH
CLATT
SSS V

Z85
-600?
PRAESOS
ABS·1906,41

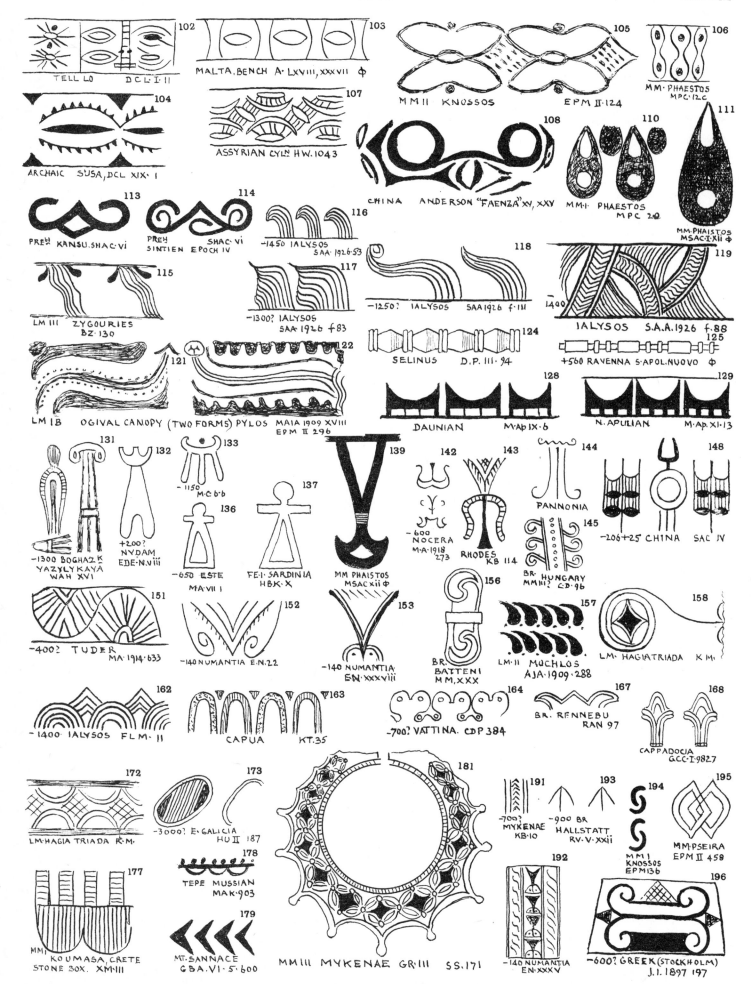

102 TELL LO DCL.I.II

103 MALTA, BENCH A. LXVIII, XXXVII φ

104 ARCHAIC SUSA, DCL XIX. I

105 MM II KNOSSOS EPM II·124

106 MM PHAESTOS MPC. 12C

107 ASSYRIAN CYLN H.W. 1043

108 CHINA ANDERSON "FAENZA" XV, XXV

110 MM·I PHAESTOS MPC 2.0

111 MM PHAISTOS MSAC·I·XII φ

113 PREH KANSU.SHAC.VI

114 PREH SINTIEN SHAC.VI EPOCH IV

115 LM III ZYGOURIES BZ·130

116 -1450 IALYSOS SAA·1926·53

117 -1300? IALYSOS SAA·1926 f·83

118 -1250? IALYSOS SAA1926 f·III

119 -1400 IALYSOS S.A.A. 1926 f.88

121 LM IB OGIVAL CANOPY (TWO FORMS) PYLOS

122 MAIA 1909 XVIII EPM II 296

124 SELINUS D.P. III·94

125 +560 RAVENNA S·APOL.NUOVO φ

128 DAUNIAN M·Ab IX·6

129 N. APULIAN M·Ap. XI·13

131 -1300 BOGHAZ K YAZYLYKAYA WAH XVI

132 +200? NYDAM EDE·N.VIII

133 -1150 M·C b·b

136 -650 ESTE MA·VII·I

137 FE·I· SARDINIA HBK· X

139 MM PHAISTOS MSAC XII φ

142 -600 NOCERA M·A·1918 273

143 RHODES KB 114

144 PANNONIA

145 BR· HUNGARY MMIII? C·D·96

148 -206+25 CHINA SAC IV

151 -400? TUDER MA·1914·633

152 -140 NUMANTIA E·N·22

153 -140 NUMANTIA E·N·xxxVIII

156 BR. BATTENI MM.XXX

157 LM·II MOCHLOS AJA·1909·288

158 LM· HAGIA TRIADA K·M·

162 -1400 IALYSOS FLM. II

163 CAPUA KT.35

164 -700? VATTINA. CDP 384

167 BR. RENNEBU RAN 97

168 CAPPADOCIA G.C.C·I·982.7

172 LM·HAGIA TRIADA K·M·

173 -3000? E. GALICIA HU II 187

177 MM·I KOUMASA, CRETE STONE BOX. XM·III

178 TEPE MUSSIAN MAK·903

179 MT. SANNACE GBA.VI·5·600

181 MM III MYKENAE GR·III S.S.171

191 -700? MYKENAE KB·10

192 -140 NUMANTIA E·N·XXXV

193 -900 BR HALLSTATT RV·V·xxii

194 MM·I KNOSSOS EPM136

195 MM·PSEIRA EPM II 458

196 -600? GREEK (STOCKHOLM) J.I. 1897 197